VALUE
AT THE
TOP

VALUE
AT THE
TOP

Solutions to the Executive
Compensation Crisis

IRA T. KAY
The Hay Group

HarperBusiness
A Division of HarperCollins*Publishers*

HarperCollins books may be purchased for educational, business, or sales promotional use. For information, please write: Special Markets Department, HarperCollins Publishers, Inc., 10 East 53rd Street, New York, NY 10022.

Designed by Irving Perkins Associates

Library of Congress Cataloging-in-Publication Data

Kay, Ira T.
    Value at the top: solutions to the executive compensation crisis / Ira
T. Kay.
        p.   cm.
    Includes bibliographical references and index.
    ISBN 0-88730-501-6
    1. Chief executive officers—Salaries, etc.—United States.
2. Executives—Salaries, etc.—United States.   3. Consolidation and
merger of corporations—United States.   I. Title.
    HD4965.5.U6K39   1992
    658.4'0722'0973—dc20   91-58497

---

92   93   94   95   96   AC/HC   10   9   8   7   6   5   4   3

To my shareholders
Sarah, Benjamin, and Jonathan

CONTENTS

ACKNOWLEDGMENTS

THE DUAL concepts that the labor market for executives is working effectively and that there may be a problem with stock options stem directly from my consulting experience over the past decade. I owe a great deal to my clients, both named and unnamed in this book, clients who allowed me the privilege of helping them think through the challenge of linking a compensation program to the creation of shareholder value. There are many other individuals I would like to thank.

My colleagues at The Hay Group have created a supportive environment for exploring these issues with my clients and for creating this book. In particular, I would like to thank Bob Ochsner, who has been my mentor in executive compensation for more than ten years. He also helped write Chapter 5 on institutional shareholders. I also appreciate the support Dave McDaniel, the head of Hay's U.S. operations and my boss, gave me while I was working on this manuscript. Rod Robinson and Diane Lerner, also from Hay, played major roles in the writing of Chapter 6 on accounting issues and Chapter 5, respectively. Other Hay people who were helpful were Ken Welde, Janine Roll, Robert Oliver, Shari Steele, and the word-processing group.

I extend my gratitude to Wally Wood for his editorial and organizational contributions to the manuscript and to Virginia Smith, my editor at HarperBusiness.

Several people were extremely helpful to me indirectly by contributing to my intellectual development. Professor

Michael Jensen at the Harvard School of Business has brilliantly and, in my opinion, uniquely portrayed the problems with the American corporation very differently than the media would have us believe. Paul Cholak (currently at Alexander & Alexander) and Gran Bowie were my bosses at Shearson Lehman and Kidder Peabody, respectively. They allowed me the freedom to try my ideas within those companies. Peter Cohen, the former chairman of Shearson, also taught me about the power of longer-term incentive plans within the corporate environment. I would finally like to thank my parents for their support on this and all my projects.

CHAPTER 1

THE WRONG CRISIS

THERE IS a crisis in executive compensation, but the critics are looking at the wrong crisis.

Most people think the problem is with compensation *levels*. They think American corporations pay their executives too much. Corporations do so—this argument runs—because the executives are greedy, out of touch with reality, and because they can get away with it.

But that is not the real crisis in executive compensation, since I will show that most executives are not overpaid relative to their performance. The problem is the particular executive behavior that too many compensation plans motivate. Stock option plans specifically motivate executives to take strategic risks—often in the form of acquisitions—that are more hazardous than the shareholders desire. By the end of this book, you'll see what's wrong with many current compensation programs—why they motivate such perilous behavior and why, if companies do not change, such behavior is likely to increase as we move through the 1990s. You will also understand exactly how the plans may be changed to align shareholder and executive interests.

To illustrate what I'm talking about, consider Steve Ross, now the co-chief executive officer of Time Warner. His compensation levels, as former chairman of Warner Communications, have become a source of media hype for what is generally wrong with American corporations.

According to *Forbes* magazine, Steve Ross earned nearly $280 million during his seventeen years as head of Warner

Communications. That's an average of almost $16.5 million a year and, by most measures, an enormous amount of money.

Was Steve Ross overpaid? How much should Warner have paid him? To understand whether Steve Ross was overpaid or not, I have to ask more questions: Did his compensation motivate him to create economic value for his shareholders? Yes! How well did Warner's shareholders do during the period Ross was CEO? Very well!

During his years as head of Warner Communications, Steve Ross created more than $10 billion in value—stock price appreciation plus dividends—for the corporation's shareholders. The stock price rose from $15 in 1973 to $83 in 1990 when Time Inc. bought the company. In that period a share of stock earned around $14 in total dividends. For his efforts, Ross received 2 to 3 percent of the total value created, much of that in the final moments of Warner's history, as Steve Ross and his board of directors negotiated an excellent deal, selling the company to Time Inc. at a large premium.

WHAT CRISIS IN EXECUTIVE COMPENSATION?

Is there a crisis in executive compensation? Unfortunately, like many complex questions, the answer is both yes and no. I call this the "duality factor of executive compensation." On the one hand, compensation always motivates changes in executive behavior. On the other, the wrong results can occur from this behavior.

No, executive compensation is not in crisis, if the crisis is whether compensation plans are motivational. Executive pay plans always motivate executive behavior. Sometimes they motivate behavior that is in the shareholders' interests, and sometimes they motivate behavior that is not. It is the responsibility of senior management and boards of directors to develop pay programs that *always* motivate executive behavior that *is* in the shareholders' interests.

Graef S. Crystal, a compensation consultant and adjunct professor at the business school at the University of California at Berkeley, says there is a crisis. His recent book, *In Search of Excess: The Over-Compensation of the American Executive*, argues that exceptional compensation levels and programs prove that there is a crisis.

But he is wrong. The huge compensation levels of specific executives—Steve Ross, Michael Eisner at Disney, and Roy Vagelos at Merck—are almost always associated with phenomenal returns to shareholders. Are there high-performing companies with relatively low paid CEOs? Yes, they are clearly the exceptions, but frequently the CEO is also the founder with huge shareholdings, such as Warren Buffet at Berkshire Hathaway and Philip Knight at Nike, where he and other insiders own 37 percent of the stock. Are there low-performing companies with high-paid CEOs? Yes, and their boards should modify the compensation plans. In any large sample, there will always be statistical "outliers," or exceptions. The question is whether pay is generally linked to performance. Our data, research, and anecdotes prove that it is. The atypical companies on which critics focus should be addressed—but they are the exceptions.

At the same time, yes, executive compensation is in crisis because, as I will demonstrate in considerable detail, stock options, a major component of most programs, have motivated executives to attempt excessively risky strategies. These strategies are not in the shareholders' best interests. They are not, surprisingly, even in the long-term interests of the executives using them.

Individual corporations and the American economy have needed very different compensation programs at different points in their history; both will need dramatically new programs for the next phase. Interestingly, it appears that Steve Ross and the Warner board of directors—and the current Time Warner board where Ross is CEO—were aware of these changing needs.

Essentially, Warner linked Ross's compensation levels to profitability and stock price increases. During the first phase, the corporation gave him regular stock options. During the second phase, he exercised these options so that by 1990, when Time Inc. offered to buy the company, he owned nearly 900,000 shares of Warner stock. During the third phase, following the acquisition, Ross received 1.8 million options on Time Warner stock, but these options had a price of $150 at a time when their stock price was $117—obviously a real inducement to try to push the stock above the $150 mark.

These programs match quite well what was truly in the shareholders' interests during those same time periods. Could Steve Ross have been motivated to create the billions in value for less money? Probably. But if in 1973 Warner shareholders had been asked, "Would you be willing to give up 2 percent of the value created in exchange for more than $10 billion?" how would they have answered? I believe they would have said, "Yes!"

Steve Ross's compensation programs and levels, although extreme, are a prototype of the executive compensation drama. His experience involves stock options, shareholder value, board of director responsibility, and a merger. How do these issues fit together, and what is their impact on the American economy?

THE COMPENSATION/TAKEOVER CONNECTION

The two most dramatic events in the American corporate world of the late 1980s and early 1990s were the simultaneous explosions in takeover activity and in executive compensation. As we've said, executives, with some exceptions, are not overpaid, and U.S. executive compensation programs have been a source of American competitive advantage. But were unnecessary takeovers related to executive compensation? They were. And to demonstrate that, I will discuss the structure and types of executive compensation, their impact on takeover activity, and the actual size and composition of compensation payouts.

This book's hypotheses are:

1. Compensation plans motivate executives.
2. An effective labor market for executives exists, one in which annual pay especially is linked to performance.
3. The proliferation of stock options (and a corresponding lack of ownership of real stock) has encouraged executives to undertake acquisitions that were not necessarily in the long-term interests of the shareholders.

While some acquisitions did deliver the promised results, most acquisitions of one company by another reduced the buying company's value. That's not what the acquiring company's management ever plans, but that's the way it tends to work out.

But why focus on compensation and "takeovers"? Takeovers, or acquisitions, are the clearest signal to the outside world of a company's strategy. There are other sources that indicate a company's strategy, such as executive interviews, press releases, stock analysts' reports, customers and suppliers, sources that talk about new products, plant openings and shutterings, new research, price modifications, and management changes. But most of these convey less information about a strategy—specifically the strategy's *risk*—than a takeover. An acquisition says to the world, "We're becoming a conglomerate," or "We're buying a supplier," or "We're buying a competitor," or whatever. If there is a connection between pay and strategy, there is no better place to look than at a company's acquisitions.

At this point, I should make my biases clear. I have been an advisor to management and boards of directors on compensation matters for fifteen years. I head The Hay Group's

Worldwide Variable Compensation Practice, which includes executive compensation, annual incentives, sales incentives, and "work force" compensation—profit sharing, gain sharing, and the like. My primary objective is to help corporations use compensation to increase shareholder value.

American management has done an excellent job of running the large corporations that are the engine of the most successful economy in the history of the world. Nevertheless, there is always room for improvement, and executive pay levels and the relationship of stock options to takeovers have disturbed me for many years. My perspective here is that of the board of directors and the senior executives. What can they do about compensation to ensure that they, executives and boards, make the best decisions about all matters, including acquisitions?

Clearly, while compensation does motivate executives, it's not the only factor that motivates them. Their company's financial health and the stock price motivate them. Other goals include power, prestige, affiliation, and the company's size. To the extent that these are aligned with the creation of value for the shareholders (stock price appreciation and dividends), there is no problem. The chief executive and his managers can pursue all these goals, and everybody wins.

However, frequently some of these other goals conflict with the creation of shareholder value. Under current economic conditions—and the early 1990s may be similar to the early 1980s—stock options often misalign these goals. Since stock options have no downside risk for the executives who have them, they can motivate a search for strategies—including acquisitions—that are riskier than the shareholders desire. Money/compensation may not be the only motivator (or even the primary motivator) of executive behavior, but it does motivate, and it is never good for the shareholders—or any owner—to have the economic interests of their employees different from their own.

The issues of executive compensation programs and corporate takeovers belong within two other contexts: the current state of executive compensation in the United States and the other causes of takeovers. Each area is fraught with mythologies.

THE MYTHS OF CORPORATE BEHAVIOR

How many people believe that American executives are greedy, overpaid, and obsessed with the short term? One does not have to be a committed socialist or unionist to think that statement contains some truth. Even *Forbes* magazine, "the capitalist tool," headlined its 1991 cover story on CEO compensation, "It Doesn't Make Sense" (that Steve Ross made $78 million in a year in which Jack Welch, the equally successful CEO of General Electric made a little over $5 million). But consider the reality and its implications.

Reality: Some American executives have created enormous economic value for their companies and ultimately for the country. At the company level, Michael Eisner at Walt Disney, while well paid by any standard ($11.2 million in 1990), received only a small percentage of the millions created for his shareholders ($820 million in profits in 1990). At the industry level, the pharmaceutical industry has invested brilliantly in the future, thereby reaping huge gains for shareholders and executives, plus job security for its employees.

Reality: The CEO of the 1980s made less (in constant dollars) than CEOs during the 1930s. Clearly, however, CEO pay needs to be much more sensitive to the companies' performance and executives must own more shares in their companies.

Reality: CEOs of top corporations are paid less than top entertainers and athletes.

Reality: The pay of top managers of American companies is not inconsistent with the pay of their European counterparts.

Here's another myth: CEOs, obsessed with being victims of hostile takeovers and improving quarterly earnings, reduce research and development and other investments in the future—all in the hope of increasing the current stock price. But what is the reality?

Reality: Takeover targets already have much lower levels of R&D than other companies. It is unlikely the takeover will be financed from reduced R&D.

Reality: Generally speaking, improving quarterly earnings by using accounting gimmicks or at the expense of long-term strategic investments does not increase stock prices.

Reality: The announcement of new R&D projects—while reducing cash and short-term earnings—generally *raises* stock prices.

Here's another common myth: Executive stock options are the best vehicle to link executive and shareholder interests. Options encourage executives to own stock or, at the very least, to increase the stock price. They encourage otherwise risk-hating executives to be more entrepreneurial.

But what is the reality?

Reality: While executive stock options worked well during the growth years in the U.S., they are not adequate for today's globally competitive world.

Reality: Most executives sell their stock the day they exercise their option.

Reality: Options link the interests of executives to shareholders only when the stock price rises, not when it falls.

Reality: Options motivate executives to undertake strategies and acquisitions that are *riskier* than the shareholders desire.

Does this mean that options are always wrong and always the wrong compensation strategy? No, it does not. Options could be appropriate for a new company because stock options operate under extremely favorable accounting rules. While the executive's base salary or bonus payments reduce reported profits, the gains on a stock option do not reduce the company's reported earnings. An employee, of course, is indifferent to whether he or she receives a $100,000 bonus or a $100,000 profit on a stock option exercise.

Many start-up and other companies have exploited this anomaly in the accounting rules, and in a turnaround situation, where cash is short, options could be a very useful tool. But, with those general exceptions, companies can obtain all the benefits of stock options and resolve some of their problems by having executives somehow own more stock by using loans or other techniques that encourage or require outright stock ownership. In a later chapter we'll see exactly how a company can do this.

Here is yet another myth: Corporations acquire other companies or divisions to diversify their company's portfolio or to create synergies with existing businesses or both. They do so to create short- or long-term value for their shareholders. Furthermore, executives are motivated to make acquisitions in the interests of their shareholders. But that is hardly the reality.

Reality: Strategies to diversify the "internal" portfolio have failed to raise stock prices; conglomerates tend to yield poor stock price performance.

Reality: Portfolio diversification is best left to individual investors who select stocks for their own portfolios.

Reality: The forecasted synergies from acquisitions have rarely covered the premium paid. Many acquisitions fail, and a large proportion end up being sold by the acquiring company.

Reality: While the shareholders of the purchased company benefit significantly, most studies show no gain to the shareholders of the *buying* company.

Reality: Executives who own large amounts of their company's stock make significantly better acquisitions than executives who don't own much stock. This latter group seems to be motivated at least partly by reasons other than creating shareholder value—for example, to increase the company's size with or without increasing profitability.

Another myth: Executive compensation plans based on accounting measures—primarily earnings per share—are required to balance out stock-based plans, which are subject to vagaries beyond the executive's control. Non-stock-based plans may be appropriate at a division level (where excellent performance by one division could be swamped by poor performance at others) or at private companies. However:

Reality: Earnings per share improvements may not reflect increases in real economic value, and frequently do not improve stock price anyway, since returns may be below the true cost of capital. The bear market of the 1970s demonstrated this.

Reality: The stock market generally rewards the creation of real economic value. Even at the division level, or at private companies, long-term incentive plans must be based on economic value and not on accounting measures.

These myths are deeply embedded in American corporate life. Take, for instance, the common wisdom that modern managers are obsessively focused on short-term performance, largely ignoring the long-term strategies that will help their companies grow and prosper. Managers who make short-term, expedient decisions are quick to point at takeover specialists and myopic, earnings-hungry investors and Wall Street analysts. Every quarter, they say, they have to produce improved earnings to keep their jobs. Yet the stock market rewards long-term investments, even if those investments reduce quarterly earnings.

Supporters of executive incentive plans—stock options, stock appreciation rights, and restricted stock—have argued that, with a greater percentage of their compensation tied to stock price, the otherwise inherently risk-fearing American executive would act more like a shareholder, taking only appropriate risks and thinking for the long term. But, contrary to popular belief, management in recent times has increasingly taken a very risky approach to their corporations' investments—often in direct opposition to their shareholders' interests. They have done so largely because of their stock options.

THE TIME FOR CHANGE IS NOW

The pressure to modify existing compensation programs increased dramatically as I wrote this book. The recent increase in shareholder activism is a direct result of disappointing stock market returns on their holdings and the lack of corresponding sensitivity to executive pay. Institutional shareholders, especially pension plans such as CalPERS (the California Public Employee Retirement System), have become active in pressuring management to improve their stock prices and financial returns and to make executive pay levels much more sensitive to their company's financial and stock market performance.

In the past, institutional investors pretty much left the companies alone. They had spectacular returns during the 1980s, primarily because the financial takeover specialists generated them. In the late 1980s, when the collapse of the junk bond and takeover markets caused the disappearance of takeover specialists, these investors became worried about future returns. Because of these economic forces, they began to assume the role of disciplining management, whereas the market for corporate control—that is, the takeover market—had done so earlier.

Although, unlike individual shareholders, institutional

shareholders are large enough to influence management, Securities and Exchange Commission rules have to a degree protected companies from such institutions. Today, institutional shareholders are putting pressure on the SEC to shift the balance of power more toward the shareholders, whoever they may be. In the meantime, these shareholders are using corporate governance—shareholder voting rights, proxy disclosure, and other techniques—to try to exert pressure on boards and managements. This reflects their serious and valid concerns over how their holdings will appreciate in the future.

Changing the way corporations pay their executives, while not guaranteeing success, will go a long way toward aligning the interests of executives and these critical large owners (and, of course, all shareholders). Voluntary changes that the board of directors and management initiate are superior to changes forced upon the corporation by its large owners or by regulatory fiat.

This book is neither an apology for nor a critical assessment of American management. I describe and evaluate the compensation alternatives that were generally available to boards of directors as one tool available to implement their overall strategies. Stock option plans—with their favorable accounting and tax treatment, their positive impact at certain times in economic history, their continued success for individual companies, and their competitive proliferation—may have represented a prudent approach for a given board at a certain time. Today, however, most companies that make strategic changes to their compensation programs beyond stock options hope these changes will benefit their shareholders, their executives, and the U.S. economy as a whole.

The second chance being offered to some CEOs and the challenge to all CEOs is to fashion business strategies that increase shareholder value. These strategies are combined with financial structures and much higher levels of executive stock ownership. This book makes and supports several points to support this broad objective:

1. Stock options, with their lack of downside risk, encourage excessively risky acquisitions.
2. Stock options have not created large amounts of executive ownership.
3. Many acquisitions of one corporation by another have failed.
4. Companies that chronically made bad acquisitions frequently became takeover targets themselves, primarily by financial takeover specialists.
5. CEOs with high levels of stock ownership made better acquisitions than CEOs with low levels.
6. High levels of executive stock ownership are linked to better levels of financial performance.

Executive compensation plans—especially stock options—played a major role in creating the takeover frenzy that occurred in the mid- to late-1980s. Options encouraged executives at corporations to buy other corporations. A disproportionate number of these takeovers failed to generate an adequate return. This failure yielded three possible outcomes: general financial distress at the buyer, since debt was probably used to acquire the target; subsequent divestiture of part or all of the target; and actual or attempted takeover of the original buyer by a third party, generally a financial takeover specialist (Kohlberg, Kravis, Roberts; Clayton & Dubilier; Carl Icahn; Carl Lindner; Victor Posner; Mesa Partners; and the like).

True, the general business atmosphere regarding acquisitions created a ripe environment in which stock options could be influential. Widely held current ideas and possibilities included strategic and intellectual support for the diversified portfolio within the corporation (Bruce D. Henderson, the former chairman of the Boston Consulting Group, argued strongly for this strategy in his consulting articles, speeches, and book, *Henderson on Corporate Strategy*). The existence of a new financial instrument, the high-yield bond ("junk bond"), allowed smaller companies and investors to harness the power of all investors to take over larger companies. The U.S. economy entered a period of transition where many industries became "low growth/high cash flow" (for example, chemicals, steel, manufacturing) and therefore ripe for takeover. It has been argued that the public corporate structure no longer works for such companies.

Moreover, highly skilled investment bankers were able to structure the deals, and investment banks were willing to take debt and equity positions in the deals. Also, commercial bankers, to earn the significant fee and interest income, were willing to lend money to these deals. Finally, a booming stock market seemed limitless.

While all this was true, executive compensation remains the primary suspect—the "secret" hiding in the closet.

Executive compensation and takeover activity have generated a tremendous amount of heat, not to mention ink, in business publications. Investors, editors, board members, and managers have given executive compensation so much attention for several reasons. While many companies are exceptions to these comments, managers and their boards must address both the reality and the perceptions of these issues. There is:

1. A shareholder quest to replicate the returns of the 1980s.
2. A social desire that everyone be held accountable for his or her actions.
3. A sense of "mind-numbing" CEO pay levels.
4. A perception of limited (or no) downside risk for executives who are betting the company, while shareholders face real risk.
5. A belief that executive pay levels dramatically higher than in other countries diminish U.S. global competitiveness.
6. A shareholder inability to challenge effectively what they perceive to be abusive practices.

7. A growing belief that the board of directors and the compensation committee are not effectively controlling the executive pay process.
8. An apparent gap between pay and performance.
9. A view that proxy disclosures regarding executive pay are incomprehensible.
10. A perception that the relationship between the CEO and the compensation committee is too close.

Critics have also attacked the takeover market. Specifically, they claim:

1. The takeovers have created ruinous amounts of debt.
2. Shareholders have not received their fair share of the wealth.
3. Great companies have been ruined or eliminated.
4. Massive layoffs will occur to pay for the debt.
5. Taxpayers will suffer.
6. Companies will reduce research and development and other critical investments.
7. Poison pills help to entrench management.
8. Golden parachutes for executives are unfair.

As I address both sets of criticism, I place the takeover craze in the context of executive compensation structure. I first discuss the problems that occur when shareholder and executive interests are not aligned. I then discuss the market for executives, because without a working labor market there can be no effective compensation programs. While compensation and the takeover craze could be separate studies, my focus will be on the appropriateness or the effectiveness of compensation and how it contributed to takeovers as a key example of business strategy, especially takeovers that were not in the long-term interest of the buying company's shareholders.

In the last three chapters, I discuss the new institutional shareholder activism in the context of executive compensation, the accounting and legal implications of the programs I'm suggesting, and finally, in some detail, programs that will better align shareholder and executive interest.

But first, let's see what has happened when executives and shareholders have had different risk profiles.

CHAPTER 2

THE PROBLEM WITH RISK WHEN IT'S A ONE-WAY STREET

IN FEBRUARY 1983, the Goodyear Tire & Rubber Company agreed to pay about $825 million in stock—twice book value —for Celeron Corporation, a natural gas transmission company. The idea was to reduce Goodyear's dependence on the automotive market, which at the time accounted for four-fifths of its sales (the other fifth was aerospace, which depended on military contracts), and to try to smooth out its quarterly earnings stream. In its diversification search, Goodyear had looked at Campbell Soup, Vicks over-the-counter drugs, and the Crum & Foster insurance agency before settling on Celeron. Vice-chairman Robert E. Mercer said at the time he expected Celeron would reduce Goodyear's dependence on the automotive market from 80 percent to 56 percent of its sales in five years.

Charles Pilliod, Goodyear's CEO, had cash compensation of $455,000, while he owned only 37,000 shares (worth $550,000) but had options on 67,000 more. His multiple of stock value to compensation, in other words, was only 1.2 to 1. Combining this with his larger option holdings meant that he had much more to gain (3 to 1) from a stock price increase than he had to lose from a decrease. Since the CEO had much more to gain than lose in this transaction, was this risk profile consistent with shareholder interests?

The stock market reacted to the Celeron acquisition by knocking three and a half points off the Goodyear stock price, a decline of 10 percent more than the general market. Obviously, Goodyear had misjudged the market's reaction to its acquisition strategy. Celeron's sales, which had dropped 23 percent to $901 million in 1982, before the acquisition, continued their plunge, falling to $762 million in 1983, the result of plentiful supply and low gas prices. The market's negative appraisal of this deal appeared correct.

Goodyear's diversification effort attracted the unwanted attention of Sir James Goldsmith, the Anglo-French financier who in early 1986 turned up as owner of 11.5 percent of the company and with plans to buy it all. As Goldsmith told *Business Week,* "I don't consider myself a manager. But restructuring, getting the company more efficient, that's what I'm good at."

Days after Goldsmith announced his interest, Goodyear revealed that Celeron was up for sale. Ultimately, the company fought off Goldsmith, buying back nearly $2 billion worth of its stock and several years later selling off virtually all nontire businesses, including Celeron, which went for a loss. In the process, Goodyear's long-term debt rose from $997 million in 1985 to $2.5 billion in 1986 and to $3.7 billion in 1990. Net profit has fallen steadily since 1987, and in 1991 the board of directors, to help Goodyear address its strategic challenges, appointed Stanley Gault CEO for three years. Gault, who had just retired as CEO of Rubbermaid, told *Fortune* after the announcement, "I'm not used to having debt, and I'm certainly not used to spending more than a million dollars a day for interest, every day of the week, even on Saturdays, Sundays, and holidays. That we cannot live with." At the end of 1991, Goodyear floated a stock offering to raise $423 million in an attempt to reduce its 60 percent debt-to-capital ratio, with the goal of getting it below 50 percent.

Was this failed acquisition a direct result of the low amount of stock owned by the executives? This, of course, is impossible to tell. Nevertheless, if I had been a Goodyear stockholder, I would have much preferred higher stock ownership by the managers before they implemented an acquisition strategy.

TOO MUCH RISK? OR TOO LITTLE?

Until now, the acquisition motives of corporate chieftains have baffled business observers. Why did so many chief executive officers make so many acquisitions that actually reduced shareholder value? Why did they take such drastic measures while at their companies' helms? Did they risk too little—or too much? Were they focused too tightly on the short term? What role did executive compensation plans play in defining the motives of corporate executives? Has the public corporation been eclipsed, or can higher leverage (debt) and more executive stock ownership yield improvements?

I believe the interests of executives and shareholders can be made identical through carefully crafted executive compensation plans. The public corporation has not been eclipsed, and higher leverage and more executive stock ownership can yield improvements.

This book is not another attack on corporate America. Quite the contrary. During the 1980s, CEOs were rationally following the strategic direction set by and with their boards of directors. This strategy was set explicitly in the form of five-year plans to diversify and implicitly in the form of stock option plans.

As is often the case in corporate affairs (not to mention human concerns in general), most people define the "correct" or prudent behavior at any given time relative to what their peers are doing. For a CEO to recommend, or for a board to approve, a strategy of low debt, no acquisitions, and no stock options would have been considered maverick during the mid-1980s.

American corporations should in fact have taken on more debt—not to make unsuccessful acquisitions but to spin off

more cash to shareholders. Certain corporate finance specialists argue that by undertaking debt, repayment becomes a
discipline that focuses the company's resources. Companies
carrying appropriate debt levels tend to use the free cash flow
in a manner that creates shareholder value instead of strategies that are uncertain at best, or that reduce shareholder
value at worst.

Corporations should have made some acquisitions, but far
fewer than they actually made—not to diversify, but acquisitions that created strong links to existing businesses, con-
nections the stock market would have rewarded, not
punished. The acquisitions should have been made at lower
premiums so that the buying company's shareholders could
have participated in the superior returns that the target company's shareholders received.

Corporations should have developed better techniques for
putting more shares into key executive hands. For had the
executives been major shareholders instead of option holders
only, they would have been motivated by prudent rather
than rash strategies. They would have made fewer (or wiser)
acquisitions, increasing the stock's value for the outside
shareholders as well as for themselves.

WHY STOCK OPTIONS HAVE FAILED

Stock options were designed to marry the interests of shareholders and executives. They have failed because *many executives don't own much stock in their companies*. They own *options*
on shares, not the shares themselves. That is, boards of directors have given executives the right to acquire a certain
number of shares at a predetermined price on a predetermined date. Hence, the conflict.

While an option holder and a shareholder have some attributes in common, they are exposed to very different risks.
Shareholders carry all the risk, while option-holding managers have nothing to lose and everything to gain by their

decisions. If the company performs well, and the stock price increases, the executives can exercise their options to buy shares at what is now a below-market price and immediately sell them for a profit. If the stock price goes down, the executives lose nothing, because they owned nothing. They simply give up the option.

Shareholders, on the other hand, are affected no matter what happens. If the stock price increases, they can sell at a profit. But if the stock price goes down, they can lose their entire investment. They are locked in.

During the 1980s, with little to lose and everything to gain, American corporate executives increasingly made high-risk acquisitions that often ended in ignominious disaster. Even when stock options worked as planned, and risky acquisitions and strategies paid off brilliantly, executives and shareholders were not operating with the best tools. Which is not to say that options never worked well. There are a number of companies for whom stock options and diversification have worked out extremely well. Perhaps the best example is General Electric, a corporation that has successfully used some of the compensation programs I criticize and that undertook a diversification strategy few other companies have easily implemented.

Confounding the odds, GE did use stock options and diversification to create enormous shareholder wealth. GE is more exception than rule, but it does prove the rule in one way. We've said that stock options motivate executives to undertake risky acquisitions and strategies. By definition this means that most such strategies will not pan out; it also means by definition that some of them will work and will pay off handsomely.

Through skillful management as well as some luck, General Electric has been extremely successful in its diversification into entertainment (NBC Television Network) and financial services. The company did have prior experience in financial services with the GE Credit Corporation, which financed dealer inventories and consumer appliance/television purchases. Other companies cannot use GE as a model because they cannot count on luck.

In today's competitive world the tool that created so much failure in the 1980s—stock options—continued to be flawed in the 1990s. Executives must have a direct and substantial ownership stake in their companies. When they do, the executives carry as much downside risk as their shareholders. When they do, as I have seen repeatedly in my consulting practice, executive behavior will change and the results can be astounding.

How Things Have Changed

When it comes to blue chips, no company is bluer than Big Blue itself, International Business Machines. At one time, IBM was America at its best—not only the greatest computer maker in the world, but the greatest company in the world. What's more, behind its mainstay—punch-card machines, typewriters, and the intimidating new things called computers that promised to revolutionize data processing—IBM had a real, human face. His name was Thomas Watson, the former National Cash Register salesman who ran IBM like an extension of his own family. In 1939, for example, when a train carrying IBMers to a company convention in New York City derailed in upstate New York, Thomas Watson, Sr. himself climbed out of bed at two in the morning, drove to the Port Jervis accident scene, and secured hospital beds for the injured and temporary lodging for the others.

Tom Watson, Sr. was the living personification of IBM. Everyone in his family owned company stock. The company urged IBM employees to buy company stock. To sell IBM stock was unheard of. When Mr. Watson retired, he passed on the reins to his sons, Tom, Jr. and Dick. It was a simple strategy, and for a long time it worked.

But things change. IBM is still the bluest of the blue chips, but battered by worldwide competition and the recession, IBM's earnings have been weak in recent quarters. For the first time in years, IBM's stock dipped below $100 a share. Things got so bad for Big Blue that Chairman William Akers rebuked his employees, chastising them for losing sight of IBM's commitment to its shareholders and to the bottom line. Even the chairman publicly took it upon himself to shoulder some of the blame.

But is Akers really carrying his fair share of the load? Sure, he's making the decisions that will determine the computer giant's future. But Akers and his fellow executives own less than 1 percent of IBM's common stock, dramatically less than the Watson family. The managers in charge of tens of billions of dollars of shareholder equity have very little of their own money on the line when they make a decision about IBM's future.

One cannot blame a low level of executive stock ownership at IBM on the executives themselves. The situation reflects the American enterprise's evolution during the twentieth century from family- and owner-managed company to professionally managed corporation. This transition offered the corporation major benefits, since second- and third-generation family members at large companies—Ford, Chrysler, RCA, Mellon, the list can be extended indefinitely —were not as capable of managing the mature companies as their grandfathers were at founding and building them.

The good news is that the professional, nonfamily members managed these behemoths more effectively than the families did. The bad news is that these professionals came with no company stock, and, with generally limited personal assets, they were in no position to purchase stock any time soon.

According to W. Liebtag, E. I. Du Pont de Nemours began bringing professional managers into the company in the early 1900s. In 1904 Du Pont implemented the first stock bonus plan in a large American company. This was the beginning of the process to try to unite the interests of share-holders and management.

American corporate executives as a whole do not own substantial direct stakes in their own companies. As Harvard scholar Michael Jensen pointed out in the *Harvard Business Review* in May 1990, "CEO share ownership has never been very high. Nine out of ten own less than 1 percent of their company stock, while fewer than one in twenty owns more than 5 percent of the company's outstanding shares." Over the years, companies have attempted to change this with stock options.

A stock option simply grants an executive the right (but not the obligation) to buy shares of the company's stock at a specified price during a fixed period of time. Giving execu-tives stock options didn't solve the problem of making them stockholders, however, because they had other personal fi-nancial priorities—first home, tuition, second home, diver-sified estate portfolio. These came before company stock ownership, and typically the executives exercised their op-tions and bought the stock only when they could immedi-ately sell it at a profit. While this practice was not universal, relatively few executives bought their stock at the option price and then held on to it through thin and thick (Warner's Steve Ross being an interesting exception to the pattern).

Today, as our figures in the chart on the following page indicate, the CEO's balance sheet shows company stock to be relatively unimportant (6 percent estimated on average), although most of the income to accumulate these assets came from W-2 income from this or a similar company.

Because they did not own much, if any, stock, these pro-fessional managers were able to follow their own agendas, even if these goals were not the shareholders'. These other goals often included growth, frequently accomplished through acquisitions, even when a growth strategy did not increase shareholder value.

I believe it is in the long-term interests of both the execu-

Assets of a Typical Chief Executive Officer

	Dollars	Percent
Real Estate	$1,000,000	15%
Personal Securities	1,250,000	19
Collectibles	300,000	5
Limited Partnerships	600,000	9
Corporate-Related Assets	3,400,000	52
Savings Plan	$ 350,000	5%
Value of Pension	1,750,000	27
Stock Owned	400,000	6
Value of Stock Options*	900,000	14
Total	$6,550,000	100%

* Present value at grant.

SOURCE: The Hay Group estimates by Robert C. Ochsner.

tives and the shareholders (and therefore the board of directors) to implement stock-based plans that allow executives less diversification. While some executives may complain initially—and some may leave for companies where maximum diversification remains available—ultimately the risk profiles of the external shareholders and the new executive shareholders will be similar. This symmetry of risk profiles creates much more effective strategies and financial performance.

EXECUTIVE OWNERS TAKE FEWER CHANCES

The point should not be underestimated. When executives own a large stake in their firms, the results can be startling. A Hay Group study found that companies in which executives have a high stock ownership turned out to be better performers than companies in which the executives own little stock. The reason is simple: The executives have their own money on the line. The company's success (or failure) affects their income directly. The Hay Group study looked at several industries—chemicals, high technology, insurance, textiles, pharmaceuticals, and banking—and in every case found a direct correlation between high executive ownership and high return on equity.

First, let's look at a comparison of two industries, one that has enjoyed a high return on equity and one that shows a low return. The CEOs of pharmaceutical companies in general own much more stock than do the CEOs of commercial banks; many of these purchases were via stock options, and therefore presumably at a discount to the market price when executives exercised the options. As the table below shows, the pharmaceutical industry's financial performance is much higher than that of commercial banking.

By the way, the figures for commercial banking include a very large purchase of stock by John Reed, chairman of Citicorp. Reed bought the stock at the market price and did not use options. This was a tremendous long-term vote of confidence in the company that may yet "pay off."

The Hay Group study also found that within the same industry, companies with CEOs as owners outpaced those in which the executives did not own much stock. The table on page 27 demonstrates this point.

The figures in that table indicate that in the textile industry, Hay found twelve public companies in which the CEOs owned on average 10.4 percent of company shares. These companies showed a return on equity of almost 17 percent. But in the six companies Hay found with lower ownership, those in which the CEO owns on average 0.36 percent of the

How Pharmaceuticals and Commercial Banking Compare

Industry	Shares Owned by CEO	Average Value of Stock to Cash Compensation	Average Three-Year ROE
Pharmaceuticals	233,000	$9: $1	+28%
Commercial Banking	117,000	$4: $1	−2%

Note: Ten largest publicly traded companies in each industry.
SOURCE: The Hay Group.

CEO Stock Ownership and Financial Performance

Industry	Number of Companies	Average Percent Owned by CEOs	Average Three-Year ROE
Textiles			
High Ownership	12	10.40%	16.60%
Low Ownership	6	0.36	7.90
Pharmaceuticals			
High Ownership	10	0.55	23.40
Low Ownership	4	0.01	15.20
Commercial Banking			
High Ownership	17	0.82	10.70
Low Ownership	28	0.07	5.40

SOURCE: The Hay Group.

shares, the return on equity was only about 8 percent. Even in commercial banking, where high ownership has to be defined as 0.82 percent stock ownership, those companies showed almost twice as high an average three-year return on equity, 10.7 percent, as those with low ownership where the return was 5.4 percent.

What's the secret of executive ownership? Risk and reward. The effective corporate chieftains have more of their money on the line, so they are tied to downside risk as much as the shareholders.

If we look at all inside executives as in the table below, not simply CEOs, we find the same pattern. Once again, high ownership is related to high levels of company financial performance.

HOW OPTIONS DIFFER FROM SARs AND RESTRICTED STOCK

Before examining what's wrong with stock options and other stock incentive programs, let's first look at exactly what they are.

Executive Stock Ownership and Financial Performance

Industry	Number of Companies	Average Percent Owned by Executives	Average Three-Year ROE
Chemical			
High Ownership	4	27.0%	17.2%*
Low Ownership	14	0.6	13.1*
High Technology			
High Ownership	23	11.3	15.7
Low Ownership	17	0.8	12.6
Insurance—Life and Health			
High Ownership	13	6.8	17.4
Low Ownership	11	0.8	10.2
Insurance—Property and Casualty			
High Ownership	10	17.5	16.6
Low Ownership	10	0.3	14.3

* Five-year average return on equity.
SOURCE: The Hay Group.

The *stock option* has been the most common form of stock incentive in recent years. As I said, it grants an executive the right to buy shares at a specified price during a fixed time period. The option is usually included as part of the executive's compensation package.

Consider the hypothetical case of a defense company's CEO who, in addition to his annual salary of $200,000, holds options to buy 5,000 shares. The contract entitles him to buy all or some of the shares at any time within five years at the price of the stock when the option is granted, say $50 per share. If during those five years, the stock's price doubles to $100, the executive could exercise his option and buy the shares from the company at $50, paying $250,000 (5,000 shares multiplied by $50), then immediately resell them on the open market for $100, for a $250,000 net profit. The executive is not required, of course, to sell the stock.

If the stock doesn't increase in value, the executive simply allows the option to expire. He loses no money. The shareholder, on the other hand, has already paid, say, $50 a share for the stock. If nothing untoward happens, and the stock price does not move upward, the shareholder makes no money when selling the stock. But if the executive—trying to drive the stock price higher—makes poorly conceived acquisitions or other bad decisions and the stock tumbles to less than $50 a share, the shareholder loses.

Stock appreciation rights, or SARs, another widely used stock incentive, show the same kind of risk-reward imbalance. An SAR gives an executive the right to receive the increase in the stock price in cash (or in stock, since SARs often pay out the profit in shares) without having to go through the bother of buying shares. Unlike options, the executive doesn't have to lay out money to purchase the stock. For the executive, it's a no-risk proposition.

Take the defense company CEO. Let's say he gets 5,000 SARs with the stock trading at $50. The stock doubles within five years, and the executive collects $250,000 (5,000 SARs multiplied by $50 per SAR). The difference this time is that the executive does not even have to actually put out $250,000 to buy the shares at his exercise price of $50 before selling them at $100. The CEO simply collects the cash or stock.

The stock appreciation right was invented because insiders, that is, officers and directors as defined under Section 16(b) of the Securities and Exchange Act, could not, until 1991, exercise their stock options and sell the stock immediately. They had to hold the stock for six months since they could be selling on inside information. This introduced an element of risk into the situation; it was possible that the stock price might go down during the six months they had to hold the stock. Indeed, it might drop below the option price so that the executive could conceivably lose real—that is, his own—money. While this real stock ownership may have been in the shareholders' interest, it was not in the executives' short-term interest.

The stock appreciation right gave the executives the cash from a stock price rise without exercising the option or holding any shares. It was a separate plan with advantages to the executive. And aside from the disadvantage to the shareholder, SAR plans had the further disadvantage of their accounting rules. Where a stock option creates no charge to earnings (since the executive's profit comes from the open market), the SAR payment is charged against profit.

SARs used to be frequently granted "in tandem" with options for top executives, that is, insiders under Section 16(b) of the securities law. This means they got either the option or the SAR. In early 1991, bowing to the argument that companies were effectively getting around the law's intent with the SAR, Congress changed the securities laws. Executives and directors may now exercise their options and sell their stock on the same day. This means the motivation for stock appreciation rights no longer exists. The shareholder interest issue remains, however; if the executives can exercise their options and sell on the same day, the option may be a way to motivate them to drive the stock price up, but it's not a way to encourage them to hold the stock for the longer term.

Restricted stock is the last major stock incentive program corporations commonly use. With restricted stock, the executive can even make money if the company's stock price goes down. Companies with sluggish stock prices use them heavily, companies whose stock options and SARs are not likely to pay off. Restricted stock is a gift of company shares, a gift that becomes more valuable with each point the stock climbs but which is worth something even if the stock declines. The restriction refers to the limitation on the stock's sale for a given time period, typically three to five years.

Take our defense company chief executive. If his 5,000 shares of restricted stock rose to $60, the executive would have title to stock worth $300,000. If the stock doubled to

$100, he would get shares worth $100 each. Even if the stock drops in value by half—to $25—the executive would still receive company stock worth $25 per share. Nothing to lose, everything to gain. Meanwhile, the shareholders who paid $50 for their stock have lost half the money.

In the past two or three years, a number of companies— Georgia Pacific, General Motors, and American Airlines among others—have dramatically improved their restricted stock plans. In 1989 General Motors paid bonuses, which had been in cash, in restricted GM stock. This conserved the corporation's cash since the corporation used stock rather than money. The change was, in effect, an involuntary stock purchase by the key management group. It reflects a major step in linking shareholders and employees, since these executives cannot sell the stock for a given period and during that time they have every interest in seeing the stock price appreciate.

The other companies also improved restricted stock by adding a performance dimension to the time restriction. If the company achieves certain financial targets, or if the stock attains a certain price level, then, and only then, will the sale restriction be lifted.

HOW SHAREHOLDER AND EXECUTIVE RISK PROFILES COMPARE

A graphic picture of the risk profile of these various plans in comparison to the external shareholder would be useful. Figures 2-1 and 2-2 show the distinction between the risk profiles of an executive option holder and an outside shareholder. The vertical "profit" axes represent the profit from holding the stock; if the stock costs $50 and rises to $60, the owner makes a $10 profit.

The horizontal "risk" axes represent the hazardousness of a company's strategy. For example, Risk 1 might be a price increase for an existing product. Risk 2 might be an acquisition of a company in a related business. Risk 3 might be a diversification strategy. Each has a payoff and a probability of success. The higher the risk, the higher the payoff, but the lower the probability of success and the greater the probability of a loss. There is a maximum expected value for the shareholders and the executives. As the figures show, since the option has no downside risk, the executives are willing to take much greater risks than the shareholders, yielding level 3 as the desired risk level.

Figure 2-1 illustrates the risk-reward profile of an executive's stock option. "Risk-reward" is actually a misnomer, because this case has no real risk. The stock option presents unlimited potential for the executive as the stock's price climbs, while risk is nonexistent, because the executive has

Figure 2-1
Executive Stock Option Risk-Reward Profile

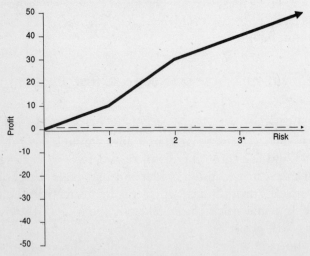

*Executive's desired risk-maximum expected value.

Source: *Handbook of Business Strategy,* 1991.

invested no capital at the time of purchase, and the option is his to exercise or not. The executive has everything to gain, and nothing to lose. Of course, there are checks on the executive's strategic decisions, mainly board approval; but within broad limitations, the board generally gives significant freedom to the CEO to set corporate strategy. Because stock options motivate executives to drive up the stock price without any downside exposure, they are more likely to employ a riskier business strategy than the outside shareholder's risk profile warrants.

Figure 2-2 illustrates the risk-reward profile of an outside shareholder. With increased risk created by the company's strategic and financial decisions, the shareholder's wealth may also increase. If the company's performance falls, however,

Figure 2-2
Outside Shareholder Risk-Reward Profile

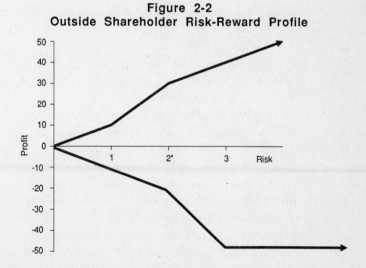

*Shareholders desired risk-maximum expected value.

Source: *Handbook of Business Strategy,* 1991.

and the fair market value of the stock declines, the shareholder can lose as much as $50 per share when the stock reaches zero—at which point the shareholder has nothing further to lose. The maximum expected value—combining the probabilities of success and failure—for the outside shareholder is level 2, below the level for the executive.

A Study in Contrasts

Continental Can and Phillips–Van Heusen illustrate these issues, the one company becoming a restructured and shrunken version of itself, the other a success. Both involve executive stock ownership, debt, the purchase and sale of assets, and the desire to create large amounts of shareholder value. Let's start with the restructuring of Continental Can.

Richard D. Hofmann, the former president of Continental Can, tells an honest yet harrowing tale of "the building up, and consequent dismantling of the Continental Group" in *Directors & Boards* magazine. As Mr. Hofmann describes it, from 1970 to 1980, the company deliberately and consciously diversified its internal portfolio, adding insurance and pipeline companies, among others. This was a time when there was considerable strategic support for matching the Boston Consulting Group's idea of cash cows, stars, and dogs—organizations with large positive cash flow but low growth, those with modest cash flow but high growth, and those with modest cash flow and low growth, respectively—to maximize returns to shareholders.

The ensuing confusion within Continental Can together with the fundamentally flawed strategy yielded significant declines in shareholder value as reflected in the stock price, which dropped from $70.125 per share in January 1970 to $27.50 in January 1980. I also believe that the stock options and low stock ownership by inside executives encouraged this flawed yet risky strategy. For example, the CEO owned only 11,000 shares but had options on 126,000 more. While clearly not the only reason for the acquisition strategy, the likelihood of a higher stock price (and therefore options with greater value), with no downside if the acquisition strategy failed, may have influenced senior managers.

In 1984 Sir James Goldsmith attempted a hostile takeover of Continental Can. The Goldsmith bid was at a 50 percent premium over the stock's market price, signaling that Goldsmith felt significant shareholder value lay hidden inside Continental Can if the acquisitions could be spun off, corporate overhead reduced, and so on. While the Goldsmith bid ultimately failed, David Murdock, another financial takeover specialist, took the company over at an even higher premium on November 1, 1984. The takeover bid incurred massive debt, which created pressure on operating results and the sale of the previously acquired companies. The Continental Can that ultimately resulted was smaller, profitable, focused, and dedicated to spinning off cash to its shareholders. While Mr. Hofmann draws many conclusions, a primary one is "few corporate managements want to admit that they should return a major portion of the cash flows to the shareholders for reinvestment." I believe that if management had owned more shares during the 1970s, Continental Can would have acquired few, if any, other companies.

For a success story, let's look at the Phillips–Van Heusen experience *Fortune* magazine reported in April 1990.

The chairman, Larry Phillips, has designed incentive plans that have clearly linked the interests of executives and owners. The eleven key employees will become very wealthy if they improve operating results and pay down debt. Each will receive $1 million if earnings grow at a 35 percent compound rate over four years. It is critical to note that the executives share in the downside risk as well—they receive no other bonus, annual or otherwise, except for the million-dollar motivator. Mr. Phillips, whose family owns 11 percent of the company, says the plan was the result of a failed takeover attempt. The company did, however, buy back $145 million worth of stock and took on significant debt.

The executives appear well on their way to receiving their

incentives. In addition to reporting positive financial results, the company's internal culture has become highly focused. For example, shirt and sweater salespeople now make joint calls to sell coordinated outfits. In addition, there are no wasteful expenses, including executive perks—no cars or country clubs. Many companies could copy P-VH's example: stock buyback, higher debt, focused culture, and high executive stock ownership plus pay that is directly linked to performance.

One more example: In May 1985 Forest Labs acquired Gilbert Labs, another company in the pharmaceutical industry. Forest Labs' CEO, Howard Solomon, owned 331,000 shares (worth $2.6 million), had only 197,000 options, and had cash compensation of $184,000. In other words, his stock to cash compensation multiple was 14.3 to 1 (to obtain this ratio, divide the worth of the executive's stock by his cash compensation), and his stock option to stock ratio was 0.6 to 1, meaning he would have had real losses from a stock price decline. At this level, management's interests are aligned with the shareholders'. When the ratio is high, management's interests are not necessarily the same as the shareholders'. As Michael Jensen has observed in May 1986, "Managers are the agents of shareholders, a relationship fraught with conflict of interest."

At the time of the acquisition, Forest Labs' stock price increased 6 percent more than the market average, reflecting Wall Street's approval of the deal. Forest Labs' sales increased from $40 million in 1985 to $141 million in 1989 (the last full year available at this writing); net profit increased from $6.8 million (or 17 percent of sales) to almost $30 million in the same period (or 21 percent of sales). The stock, which split two for one in 1986, split again in 1991. All in all a very creditable performance.

During the 1980s, Hay Group data on executive compensation programs found that the use of stock options and other programs and the size of the grants (that is, the number of options) increased significantly. If executive cash compensation had increased less than inflation, one could argue that the executives "paid for" these long-term programs as their cash declined and opportunity increased, leaving total cost constant.

To the contrary, I found that during the 1980s, executive cash compensation—base salary and bonus—increased by more than 9 percent per year, well in excess of inflation. Total cost, or total direct compensation, which includes base salary plus annual bonus plus the value of long-term plans (options), also increased by around 9 percent. While executives may have been worth these higher levels, the mix of cash and stock-based opportunity was wrong from a motivational and risk perspective.

ACQUISITIONS AS RISKY STRATEGY

Mergers and acquisitions (M&A) exploded in the second half of the 1980s. Figure 2-3 displays the level of M&A activity in billions of 1990 dollars since 1975. Note that this is a logarithmic scale; the distance from $25 billion to $100 billion is as great as from $100 billion to $400 billion.

Figure 2-3 makes two key points:

1. M&A activity rose almost steadily from 1975, jumping dramatically beginning in 1984.
2. M&A activity began declining in 1989.

As the financial takeover specialists—Kohlberg, Kravis, Roberts; Carl Icahn; Carl Lindner; Victor Posner; Ronald Perelman; and others—have withdrawn from the market, M&A activity has dropped. However, corporate buyers are still active, and Michael Jensen predicts in the summer 1991 issue of *Journal of Applied Corporate Finance* that they will become more active as the possibility of being taken over themselves by financial takeover specialists has been reduced.

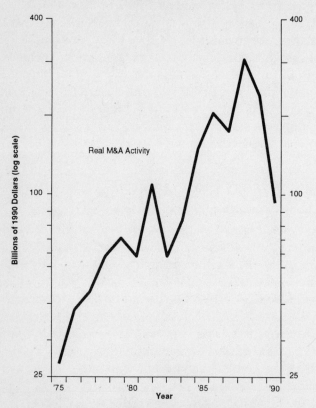

Figure 2-3
Mergers and Acquisition Activity, 1975–1990

Source: *Business Week*, "R&D Scoreboard," annual; and Merrill Lynch,
Mergerstat Review: 1990, "Corporate Control and the Politics of Finance,"
Journal of Applied Corporate Finance, 1991.

I say that different executive compensation plans can reduce the probability of bad acquisitions by corporate buyers should they become more active.

Jensen argues that ". . . takeovers today are likely to revert to the pattern of the 1960s and 1970s, when large companies used takeovers of other companies to build corporate 'empires' . . . and if the past is a reliable guide, many such acquisitions are likely to end up destroying value and reducing corporate efficiency."

People who read the *Wall Street Journal* believe they know why mergers and acquisitions took off in the 1980s. The credit goes to the emergence of the market for junk bonds, almost singlehandedly created by a bookish, ex-cheerleader from California named Michael Milken. Working his way up at Drexel Burnham Lambert in the 1970s, Milken tapped into the latent demand for high yields by peddling "fallen angels," the once investment-grade bonds of companies that had met with hard times. Milken discovered that investors were attracted to the high yields—upwards of 20 percent—offered by these once-neglected bonds, and he created the original issue, high-yield or junk bond, paying interest well in excess of staid Treasury notes and bills.

As demand grew, smaller companies and corporate raiders (aka financial takeover artists or takeover specialists), shut off from traditional sources of financing because of their lack of credit rating, came to Milken. Backed by the financier's extensive network of junk bond buyers and sellers, corporate takeover artists issued billions of dollars in such bonds. Companies the size of Rhode Island were able to gobble up corporations as big as China. People like oilman T. Boone Pickens, Reliance Group's Saul Steinberg, Revlon's Ronald Perelman, and casino czar Steve Wynn built empires with the backing of Milken's junk bonds.

This is the common wisdom. But *Wall Street Journal* readers missed the role played in merger mania by executive compensation plans. Had these plans been effectively designed, many of the decade's more disastrous corporate mergers might never have taken place. *These raiders were frequently taking over companies that had themselves executed poor acquisitions.*

These financial takeover specialists must be distinguished

from more traditional corporate buyers. They had some things in common, but their fundamental goals were very different. The financial takeover specialists looked at a relatively short time period to increase the value for all shareholders, especially and primarily themselves. The corporate "strategic" buyers were theoretically interested in a longer-term, strategic fit between their companies and the companies they were buying.

It turned out that the labels were reversed. The financial takeover specialists created economic value, and the corporate buyers ultimately ended up reducing value through their acquisitions, frequently divesting them or being taken over themselves. These corporate buyers thought they could create long-term synergies by combining what they had with what the acquisition would have—a distribution system or products or worldwide networks. But even if those strategies had merit, they overpaid for the companies they bought, paying a premium that was typically debt financed and impossible to recoup through cost savings, improved productivity, or greater sales.

As we saw in the last chapter, a widely held myth is that executives are forced to concentrate on the short term—on their daily stock price—because the ocean is swarming with sharks waiting to attack at the first sign of weakness. Further encouraging this "short-term" executive mentality was the fact that large institutions dominated share ownership. Pension funds, insurance companies, and large mutual fund conglomerates like Fidelity were always ready to tender their shares to any hostile takeover artist who offered even a small premium over the company's market price.

These institutions, in contrast to comparatively loyal individual shareholders, were under constant pressure to "churn" their stock portfolios, selling at the slightest sign of weakness to remain competitive with other money managers and to provide their customers a high return. Presumably, beleaguered "short-term" managers had to focus on getting their stock price up to ward off raiders, neglecting long-term investments in research and development or building brand name. And woe to the executive who took his eye off the stock price to invest in some long-term research. At the slightest sign of money going out the window, Wall Street reacted with its legs, as investors sold out their company stock. This conventional wisdom combines two distinct—and diverging—labels.

HOW MANAGERIAL AND MARKET MYOPIA DIFFER

Michael Jensen distinguishes between *managerial* myopia and *market* myopia in the *Journal of Economic Perspectives:* "It has been argued that, far from pushing managers to undertake needed structural change, growing institutional equity holdings and the fear of takeovers cause managers to behave myopically and therefore to sacrifice long-term benefits to increase short-term profits." This is not true, and it confuses two positions, one of which is wrong:

1. Managers are myopic and make short-term decisions.
2. Markets are myopic and overvalue short-term results.

Jensen believes that managers *do* act myopically but that there is a great deal of evidence that markets do *not*. For example, pharmaceutical companies, especially biotechnology firms, consistently invest for the long term and their stock prices go up. A study by John J. McConnel and his associates found that the stock price *rises* when a company announces new investments.

For more evidence, just look at the results of the 1985 Securities and Exchange Commission study, "Institutional Ownership, Tender Offers, and Long-term Investments." The study developed empirical tests to see whether there was indeed a relationship between institutional ownership and the short-term mentality of managers. Based on these tests, the authors concluded that there is no support for the short-term argument.

Recently Alan Murray reported in the *Wall Street Journal* that Michael Jacobs, a former director of corporate finance at the U.S. Treasury, had written *Short-Term America* (Harvard Business School Press). At the Treasury, Jacobs looked at the ways U.S. capital markets force companies to focus on short-term results at the expense of long-term competitiveness. The book argues, writes Murray, "that the short-term obsession of American companies—'business myopia' Jacobs calls it—grows out of a widening split between the people who finance American businesses and those who run them. In Germany and Japan, Jacobs notes, the providers of capital, particularly big banks, are actively involved in the management of companies and are therefore committed to their long-run viability. In the U.S., shareholders and bondholders feel no such obligation, buying and selling securities like commodities and playing little role in management."

Jacobs suggests changing securities regulations to increase the ability of large institutional investors to appoint corporate directors, writes Murray: "If such investors had more of a voice in running the company, Jacobs argues, they would be less inclined to sell their shares to the first takeover artist that comes along. He also proposes measures to tie executive pay more closely to long-term performance."

There are no data to support the idea that institutional ownership of a company encourages a low level of (or a reduction in) expenditures on research and development. Quite the contrary, it appears that high institutional ownership is linked to high research and development spending. This seems to indicate that institutional investors do take the long-term view when investing in a stock.

Firms that have been subject to hostile takeovers have had lower-than-average expenditures on research and development. Target firms spent an average of 0.77 percent of their revenue on research and development, while the control group spent 1.6 percent on research and development during the study period. "This data strongly suggests that investments in long-term projects such as R&D do not make a firm vulnerable to takeovers," say the 1985 SEC study's authors.

Institutional ownership in firms that were subject to hostile takeovers during the study period was 19.3 percent, which was about 14 percentage points lower than the 33.7 percent institutional ownership in the industry control group. This leads to the conclusion that executives of target firms were not under abnormal pressure from institutions to think short term.

And does the stock market itself frown on long-term investment? Continues the SEC: "Stock price evidence reveals that the capital market positively values companies that announce they are embarking on an R&D project." The SEC study concludes, "This evidence strongly *rejects* the proposition that the stock market values short-term earnings and not expected future earnings." It is fatal for managers to try to prevent a takeover by increasing short-term earnings at the expense of projects with positive net present value.

As I will show in Chapter 4, corporate buyers have also tried to increase their stock prices by buying other companies—a strategy that has generally failed. As one result, however, corporate raiders saw an opportunity to profitably dismantle these weakened corporate buyers themselves. They bought the companies whole and sold the assets piecemeal, in effect "unwinding" the previous acquisition strategy.

WHY EXECUTIVES MADE ILL-CONCEIVED ACQUISITIONS

So if hostile raiders and fickle institutional investors did not drive executives to embark on the ill-conceived strategies, including acquisitions, of the 1980s, what was it? A large part of the blame can be traced to the lack of executive ownership and to compensation plans that encouraged corporate leaders who had no money of their own on the line to make risky moves.

In fact, my research has found that executives under poorly designed stock options plans undertook more risks in their strategies and in their acquisitions than the shareholders would ultimately desire. At the risk of belaboring the point, they had nothing to lose and everything to gain.

This reinforces my conviction that executives need to be encouraged through their compensation plans to make optimal long-term investments. If they try to maximize short-term earnings by cutting back on long-term investment and R&D, they will fail. On the other hand, if they make risky acquisitions, they will also fail because they will ultimately punish their stock price, which will in turn attract a corporate (or financial) buyer.

In either case, there must be an optimum course for executives to follow. They must make appropriate strategic and long-term investments that balance the company's short- and long-term needs, as well as balance their interests with those of the shareholders. As we will see in Chapter 7, the search for this delicate balance is difficult and requires compensation plans that give executives a direct, long-term stake in their companies.

In the 1990s, executive compensation plans will be more crucial than ever because the days of the financial takeover specialist are over. Mike Milken is in jail, the junk bond market is a shell of its former self, and many states are enacting strict anti-takeover measures. This means that shareholders can no longer count on raiders to do their dirty work, to uncover hidden value and bring wasteful CEOs to account for their actions.

The 1990s will bring a lot more "strategic alliances," like the merger of Time Inc. and Warner Communications, that management believes will increase shareholder value, but the market says will not. With no pressure from outsiders such as financial takeover specialists, it is imperative for shareholders and boards of directors to influence corporate leaders from within, by creating executive compensation plans that make the executives share the risk, that make them own substantial, direct stakes in the firms they guide. This will ensure that a corporation will undertake these strategic alliances only if there exists a very high likelihood of success that the market will support them. This will be in the long-term interests of the executives as well.

It does not take a major restructuring to marry the risks of shareholders with those of management. Long-term incentive programs, effectively designed and judiciously administered, can do the trick. The challenge of the 1990s, then, is to fashion new approaches to executive compensation that create wealth for executives only as shareholder wealth increases at an equal rate. The secret is to give executives as much downside risk as the shareholders carry.

But before exploring what an ideal compensation plan would look like, I want to address two questions: Are executives overpaid? Did executive compensation play a role in the takeover craze?

CHAPTER 3

THE CEO LABOR MARKET: IS THERE PAY FOR PERFORMANCE?

*On the average, compensation policies
encourage executives to act out on behalf of their
shareholders and to put in the best managerial
performance they can.*

—KEVIN MURPHY

AMERICA'S FUTURE economic growth will require a different type of executive labor market than we have had. That labor market will, in turn, require a more balanced approach to risk sharing between executives and shareholders than previously existed. That market has begun to form as corporations, including their boards of directors and their key executives, explore alternatives to the standard stock option programs they have historically used. These new approaches require a number of perspectives: understanding what happened in executive compensation in the 1980s; understanding the alternative programs currently available to companies; and understanding the other factors behind corporate takeovers. These new compensation programs will improve the overall quality of managerial decisions, not just those involving acquisitions.

But is there a labor market for executives that functions in any meaningful sense of the term? A "duality" exists in the CEO labor market. On the one hand, a reasonably fluid market operates that, in general, motivates the executives. On the other, the most prevalent form of CEO compensation program, stock options, while always motivating, may not always encourage the long-term creation of shareholder value.

Anecdotes and statistics will show that large stock options and low stock ownership influenced executives to undertake overpriced acquisitions. They will also show that, in sharp contrast, companies in which the top executives held relatively few stock options or large amounts of stock executed successful acquisitions as well as other successful business strategies. However, our premise—that poorly designed executive compensation programs offered the conditions for unsuccessful and overpriced acquisitions—requires that an executive labor market exist, albeit malfunctioning. Most critics of executive pay argue there is no such market.

While business critics have always attacked executive pay, the criticism seemed to become more strident and widespread in the late 1980s and early 1990s. *Industry Week* magazine headlined a June 1988 article, "The Top Man Gets Richer," with a subhead, "As pay gaps widen between the CEO and most others in the company, the furor roars on over whether top executives are worth what they're paid." *Business Month* headed an October 1990 article with: "Compensation: The million-dollar-a-year CEO is fast becoming a public enemy. It's now time for America's executives to ask, How much is enough?" *Business Week* picked up the question in May 1991: "Investors, employees, and academics are asking, How much is enough?" and ran an editorial in the same issue, "Executive Pay: Time for Restraint." The editorial writer observed, "Last year's $1.9 million average pay for U.S. CEOs seems out of whack with corporate performance, employee sacrifices, and the whole tenor of these recessionary times. Predictably, many shareholders and employees are fed up, and even customarily inert institutional investors are exasperated.

It's time for corporate boards to face up to the growing public concern over executive pay. If they don't, a backlash against business could easily develop."

How effective can a labor market be that pays $1.9 million per person? Business writers and institutional investors ask about the sensitivity of pay for performance at specific companies. At the 1991 ITT shareholders' meeting, for example, as described in the *Wall Street Journal,* a woman asked CEO Rand V. Araskog for three valid reasons why he deserved to have his 1990 compensation more than double to $11.4 million when profit rose only 4 percent. The same article quoted individual shareholders saying about the compensation, "It's wrong! It's unjustified" and "I'm a bit insulted . . . I don't think it takes a genius to sell off assets" to boost earnings.

These critics wonder about the link between executive and shareholder interests. They attack American compensation levels relative to their European counterparts. Basically they argue, as I do here, that the shareholders bear all the risk and the executives receive all the gain.

There are, unfortunately for their shareholders, a few companies that do not link financial performance to executive pay. Those companies, however, are more rare than the popular press would have its readers believe. Most companies do indeed pay for performance. In addition, executive compensation programs strongly motivate the executives affected by the programs *even if those programs encourage decisions that are not in the best long-term interests of the shareholders.* This is the malfunction that I mentioned previously.

I will show that while it has its problems, there is an effective CEO labor market.

1. Executive pay, while high relative to much smaller jobs, is consistent with the risk and responsibilities that executives face. Further, executive pay is modest relative to that of entertainers and athletes, people with much less impact on the economy.

2. U.S. executive compensation levels are consistent with international standards.

3. Annual compensation plans, especially bonuses for CEOs, are sensitive to a company's short-term performance and have worked effectively to link executive and shareholder interests.

4. A company may use a vast array of long-term compensation programs, including stock options. Options, however, inadvertently prompt executives to undertake risky strategies, especially acquisitions (see Chapter 4). Long-term compensation plans are effective motivators, but unless the designers trace the logical outcome of any given incentive plan, they may find unintended consequences. The plan motivates the executives and changes their behavior, but not in the intended direction. Inadequate long-term incentive plans, especially stock options, are effective motivators but ineffective in their ultimate outcome.

5. High-performing companies have very different compensation programs than do lower-performing companies.

6. Senior executives, especially CEOs, do lose their jobs and are subject to a fluid labor market.

How Supply and Demand Affects CEOs

For a CEO labor market (or for any position) to exist, it must have at least one of the attributes of a market—namely, supply and demand, which rises and falls with changes in prices.

In a labor market, supply covers both the quantity of labor (number of employees, years worked, weeks worked, hours worked) as well as the quality of labor (productivity, experience, education, training, and any other attribute that would be associated with higher levels of labor contribution).

Demand in a labor market covers the type and number of jobs that companies, industries, and, in the aggregate, the entire economy or society require.

Any market, including a labor market, does not have to function perfectly for a society, or any group of participants, to achieve the benefits a marketplace economy offers over other ways to allocate scarce resources. These other forms include a socialist or planned marketplace at the macroeconomic level or some form of noncompetitive market, such as a monopoly or oligopoly, at the microeconomic level, where there *is* no social benefit. An oligopoly is a market characterized by a few suppliers who can influence prices by restricting supply. Perfect competition, on the other hand, has a large number of suppliers who take whatever prices they can get.

It is possible of course to have a monopoly or oligopoly and retain social benefits. The electric utility industry is an example of a monopolistic industry where social benefit exists, requiring the government to participate in the industry's rate-setting process. Under many other circumstances, social benefits disappear as oligopolies develop. Examples that clearly benefit private individuals without any obvious social benefit in the supply side of a product market include cartels such as OPEC.

An example of a private benefit monopoly or oligopoly in the supply side of the *labor* market would be a union hiring hall, where the union controls participation in the hall by restricting membership, and controls allocation of the jobs to the requesting employers, a construction crew, for instance. This allows the union to set the price of labor within a broad range. Obviously, if wages become so high that construction becomes very expensive, requiring contractors to charge very high sale prices or rents, construction in the community will eventually slow or stop. In other industries—textiles, shoe manufacturing, electronic assembly—the jobs may move to another community or even to another country.

One criticism of both executive compensation and the takeover craze is that they damaged the U.S. economy's efficiency. But is the criticism valid? Figure 3-1 examines the

Figure 3-1
U.S. Productivity, 1950–1989

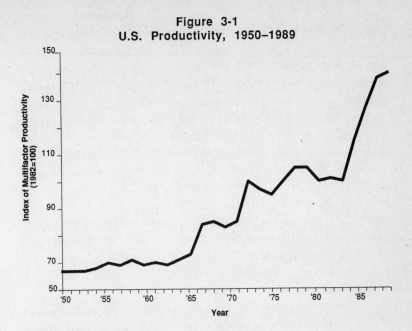

Source: *Journal of Applied Corporate Finance*, Summer 1991.

productivity levels of the U.S. economy during the period of the explosion in takeovers.

Clearly, productivity increased dramatically during the last half of the 1980s. With 1982 as an index of 100, multifactor productivity rose to almost 150 by 1989. Multifactor productivity, a measure of productivity improvements to both people and equipment, is real output per unit of combined capital and labor. While it would be difficult to prove that executive compensation and the numerous changes in corporate ownership improved productivity, there is no reason to believe they damaged the American economy. If they had, productivity would have fallen.

Critics of the executive labor market argue that this market is not working properly. They almost always mean that pay is not sensitive to performance. On the television show "60 Minutes" in November 1991, Graef Crystal stated this lack of sensitivity as follows: High performing companies have to pay well to reward their executives; poor performing companies have to pay well to keep their executives from leaving. In both cases, the executives are paid well.

The critics say that while pay may increase with high levels of, or improvements in, performance, pay almost never goes down with low levels of, or declines in, performance. They could support this thesis by comparing compensation across companies and finding that higher-performing companies do not pay better than poorer-performing companies; or by comparing compensation levels between countries and finding that American executives are paid much more than their European counterparts. My data categorically reject the notion of a poorly performing market.

To place this in economic terms, these critics are saying that executives participate in a monopolistic labor market in the United States (similar to the union hiring hall) where supply is curtailed and price therefore is higher than a pure market rate would reflect. The quality component of the executive labor supply is critical. If industry pays two executives identically, one an outstanding performer and the other a poor performer, the market is essentially paying a fixed wage without regard to the supply. It is, in other words, a monopoly just like the electric utility or the union hiring hall. Just as in the union, the beneficiaries are private individuals at the expense of the employing company and the shareholders.

WHAT ABOUT PAY FOR PERFORMANCE/MOTIVATIONAL ISSUES?

So the question is, Do executives improve their performance based upon their compensation programs? How do compensation programs at high-performing companies differ from those at poorly performing companies? Do executives change their behavior based upon the executive compensation programs under which they operate?

One of this book's key assumptions is that executives are in fact motivated by their compensation programs, indicating an effective labor market. As I've suggested, other factors do drive executives; these range from being associated with a successful company to increasing their own power and prestige through their company's size. Nonetheless, a key question is how and whether executive compensation programs motivate—that is, change—behavior. The "how," if it does indeed work, is fairly straightforward. Executives will make decisions that maximize their own personal goals—personal wealth, prestige, power, and so on—in addition to maximizing shareholder wealth. Unless the executive's goals are identical to or aligned with those other aspects of the utility function, there will be conflicts of goals.

Many studies in corporate finance have indicated that revenue growth does not necessarily indicate improved profitability. It could be in the executive's interest to manage a larger company—it's more exciting and the compensation levels usually go up. Executives always want to increase shareholder value, but they also want growth. The shareholders are interested only in shareholder value. So a conflict may arise between the growth and the profitability goals.

Figure 3-2 presents data for fifty large American corporations on the relationship between annual incentives and financial performance. The first set of bars indicates that a 20 percent increase in profits was associated with a 17 percent increase in the annual incentive payment paid to the chief executive officer. Conversely, a 20 percent decline in profits—the last set of bars—was associated with a 19 percent decline in the CEO's incentive. This reflects the sensitivity between changes in profitability and changes in annual incentives.

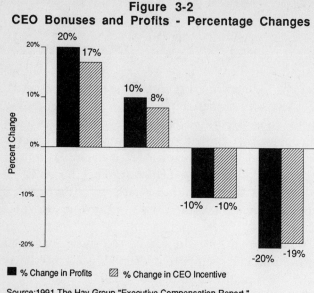

Figure 3-2
CEO Bonuses and Profits - Percentage Changes

■ % Change in Profits   ▨ % Change in CEO Incentive

Source:1991 The Hay Group "Executive Compensation Report."

The 1991 Hay Group "Executive Compensation Report" revealed numerous instances in which CEOs' annual incentives changed as a direct result of their organizations' change in profits. Although the individual amounts certainly varied, in the aggregate, percent change in CEO incentives was proportional to the percent change in organization profits.

In a thorough study of 1,200 large U.S. corporations, Kevin Murphy concluded that the critics of executive compensation are taking a highly emotional view of the labor market for executives, and are fundamentally wrong in their conclusion that executives are getting "the most for allegedly doing the least." Murphy's results, published in the *Harvard Business Review,* are worth quoting in detail:

- The pay and performance of executives are strongly and positively related.

- Compensation proposals like short- and long-term incentive plans and golden parachutes actually benefit rather than harm shareholders.
- Changes in SEC reporting requirements and a shift toward performance-based long-term compensation explain most of the apparent compensation "explosion." This shift links compensation closely to shareholder wealth and motivates managers to look beyond next quarter's results.

His data showed a strong positive relationship between increases in shareholder wealth and increases in cash compensation.

The table below summarizes the most dramatic results of Murphy's study:

How Shareholder Returns Compare to Executive Increases

AVERAGE ANNUAL INCREASE FROM 1980 TO 1984

Total Return to Shareholders	Increase in Salary and Bonus
Less than −20%	0.4%
−20–0	4.9
0–20	9.2
20–40	11.6
More than 40	16.6
Entire sample	8.8

SOURCE: *Harvard Business Review*, March–April 1986.

This study provides significant support for the hypothesis that executive compensation is motivating and, in this case, supports shareholder interests. It is important to point out, however, that one of this book's major themes is that stock options, as a major source of potential compensation, are not always and universally in the shareholders' interests. The Murphy study looked only at cash compensation. In a study of 1990 compensation levels reported in *Fortune* magazine, Graef Crystal found CEO pay—including large amounts of long-term incentive compensation (stock options)—to be almost completely unrelated to total return to shareholders. Performance differences between companies explained only 4 percent of the compensation, whereas size differences explained 15 percent. These two studies support my two major themes:

- *Cash* compensation *is* highly related to performance.
- Higher levels of *total* compensation (including stock option values) are *not* associated with higher returns to shareholders. We argue that the options are motivating riskier strategies, which, on the average, are not paying off.

Is there a difference between the compensation programs at high-performing companies and low-performing ones? A Hay Group study of the pharmaceutical industry posed this exact question.

To examine performance among participants in the Hay study, we compared the financial data from each participating organization to *Fortune* magazine's 1991 analysis of overall pharmaceutical industry financial performance in 1990. We compared each organization's measures for sales growth, return on sales, return on assets, and return on stockholders' equity to the published industry median values, and we classified each organization as follows:

High Performer—above median for all four financial measures.
Low Performer—below median for all four financial measures.
Indeterminate Performer—a combination of rankings, some above and some below industry median.

We then examined all aspects of compensation policies and practices separately for each group and compared the results for the six companies in the "high-performer" category with the five in the "low-performer" group. This comparison yielded the following characteristics of the high-performance group:

1. All these companies have competitive base salaries. Comparison of base salaries across standard job-content levels yields an average difference of only 0.2 percent between the high-performance and low-performance companies. In addition, comparison of salary administration policies and practices yields no substantial differences between the two groups.

2. The high-performance organizations offer great annual incentive opportunity than their counterparts in the low-performance group. On average, high-performance organization targets exceed those in the low-performance group by 2 percent of salary at the supervisory/other exempt level, and by 5 percent of salary at the executive level.

3. While all but one of the organizations in each performance group provide both short-term and long-term incentives, high-performance organizations provide long-term incentives to a broader group of exempt personnel. While one-third of the long-term incentive plans in the high-performance category extend below the middle manager level to supervisory and other exempt employees, none of the programs in the low-performance group extend below the middle management level.

4. Comparison of the compensation mix for the two groups reveals that, on average, incumbents in the high-performance group have a greater portion of their total remuneration package at risk. High-performance organizations place more emphasis on at-risk incentive compensation (40 percent versus 35 percent) and less emphasis on fixed base-salary payments (40 percent versus 47 percent).

This difference in incentive compensation emphasis is even more pronounced among top executives in the two groups. As Figure 3-3 illustrates, average compensation at risk for

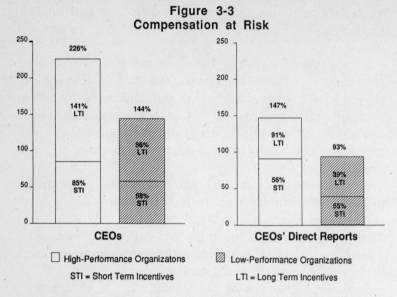

Figure 3-3
Compensation at Risk

Source: 1991 The Hay Group "Executive Compensation Study" of the Pharmaceutical Industry.

CEOs in the high-performance group amounts to 226 percent of base salary, as compared with 144 percent for CEOs in low-performance organizations. For the CEOs' direct reports, average compensation at risk falls to 147 percent and 93 percent for high-performance and low-performance group employees, respectively.

Although this sample is small and I cannot prove causality, these results imply that the concept of "pay for performance" is working in this high-performing group of pharmaceutical companies.

In many circumstances, especially when a company uses financial or accounting measures as part of an annual incentive plan, the executives can in fact improve the short-term operating results of the company. In a 1985 study of annual incentives, Hassan Tehranian and James F. Waegelein found that the announcement of a new annual incentive plan increased the announcing company's stock price by 11 percent more than it would have been without such an announcement.

My own consulting experience supports the idea that a direct link between annual compensation and corporate financial performance causes executives to focus directly on those financial measures and to take steps (revenue enhancement, cost cutting, and the like) to improve them. While there are always events outside management's control, improved annual operating results generally accompany these plans. The question is whether improving annual operating results year after year is indeed attainable.

One frequently mentioned reason for implementing a long-term incentive plan is to create a balanced perspective for the executives. Boards and shareholders fear that executives will be so highly motivated by their annual (or short-term) incentive plans that they may not make the best long-term decisions. They hope that executives will make the long-term investments that will increase the firm's net present value. If no long-term incentive plan exists, it will not be in the executives' long-term interests to make those investments. This is true because long-term investments are subtracted from annual earnings, thereby reducing annual earnings and reducing the executive's annual bonus proportionately or more (since many incentive plans are highly leveraged, they pay off poorly for performance somewhat below target and extremely well for performance above target). Executives who have only an annual incentive plan are remarkably sensitive to incremental costs, including investments that would reduce annual earnings or profits. While well-intentioned executives will generally act in the interests of their shareholders despite the impact on their own economic interests, it is always superior to try to align both shareholder and executive interests. This is the economic rationale for a long-term incentive plan that creates an economic balance valuable to all parties.

Why Executive Supply Is Not Fixed

From a quantitative perspective, there are only 500 "openings" for CEO positions among the Fortune 500 companies, so demand is fixed at 500. But is the supply fixed at 500? Absolutely not. Sources of supply include executives below the CEO level at those companies; board members; CEOs and executives at smaller or at European companies; executives below the CEO level at other companies; and consultants.

Stanley Gault, the current CEO of Goodyear Tire, was a board member of Goodyear (and retired CEO of Rubbermaid). Robert Louis-Dreyfuss, a French national, became CEO of Saatchi & Saatchi Advertising. Lawrence Bossidy, formerly vice-chairman of General Electric, became CEO of Allied Signal. And Michael Carpenter, formerly with the Boston Consulting Group, is CEO of Kidder Peabody.

The executive labor market is functioning quite well in both qualitative and quantitative terms; it is not a monopoly or a union hiring hall. Search committees have too many possibilities. While the situation can always be improved and while there are clearly companies that are exceptions to this broad labor market, the price of executive talent clearly varies with the supply (from both a quantitative and a qualitative perspective). Executives lose their jobs, and many change companies. Further, they supply a quality of labor in the form of their strategic decisions and their overall financial performance that varies with the executive compensation levels and programs under which they operate.

Current Levels of Executive Pay

What are the current levels of executive compensation? We would like to know the fixed proportion of total compensation compared to the proportion that represents opportunity, that can vary with performance. How does CEO pay compare with that of entertainers and athletes? How does executive pay compare on an international basis?

Our data suggest an executive labor market that is operating reasonably effectively. Executive pay is quite high, but this is appropriate compensation given the risks the individuals operate under and given the tremendous values that they can create. Michael Jensen and Kevin Murphy in a 1990 *Harvard Business Review* article reported that despite the headlines, top executives are not receiving record salaries and bonuses. "Salaries and bonuses have increased over the last 15 years, but CEO pay levels are just now catching up to where they were 50 years ago. During the period 1934 through 1938, for example, the average salary and bonus for CEO of leading companies on the New York Stock Exchange was $882,000 (in 1988 dollars). For the period 1982 through 1988 the average salary and bonus for CEO of comparable companies was $843,000."

Pay levels of executives reflect the company's size. The larger and more complex the organization, generally the more it costs to attract executives with the appropriate experience to manage them. Nevertheless, there is broad-based pay for performance, especially in annual incentive plans. The following tables show the average levels and mix of compensation for ten key executive positions from the 1991 Hay Group "Executive Compensation Report."

Total direct compensation, the fourth column in the tables, includes base salary plus annual bonus plus present value of long-term incentives. Because it is somewhat technical, I have put the explanation of how we value long-term incentive plans into an Appendix. It is essential to point out that the value we place on long-term plans is an opportunity not an achievement. The actual income the executive receives will depend on future financial or stock price performance.

The tables' final column, total leverage, includes annual

and long-term incentives as a percentage of salary. If an executive's salary is $100,000 and his annual bonus and long-term incentives are $200,000, the total leverage is 200 percent ($200,000 ÷ $100,000 x 100%).

Chief Executive Officer
246 Incumbents

Size of Company (revenue)	Base Salary ($000)	Total Annual Cash Compensation ($000)	Total Direct Compensation ($000)	Total Leverage
Over $5 Billion	$771.2	$1,304.3	$3,741.3	419%
$1.5 Billion to $5 Billion	542.6	766.9	1,189.2	129
$500 Million to $1.5 Billion	380.5	543.5	623.5	84
$150 Million to $500 Million	307.2	419.6	562.2	100
Under $150 Million	197.7	255.4	268.6	64

Chief Operating Officer
106 Incumbents

Size of Company (revenue)	Base Salary ($000)	Total Annual Cash Compensation ($000)	Total Direct Compensation ($000)	Total Leverage
Over $5 Billion	$553.4	$852.1	$1,662.7	217%
$1.5 Billion to $5 Billion	373.9	492.3	698.3	91
$500 Million to $1.5 Billion	277.3	357.1	387.1	59
$150 Million to $500 Million	239.9	303.9	441.1	86
Under $150 Million	159.7	226.2	242.5	53

Chief Financial Officer
285 Incumbents

Size of Company (revenue)	Base Salary ($000)	Total Annual Cash Compensation ($000)	Total Direct Compensation ($000)	Total Leverage
Over $5 Billion	$317.2	$460.0	$779.9	152%
$1.5 Billion to $5 Billion	233.2	327.8	493.8	111
$500 Million to $1.5 Billion	172.6	216.5	251.0	64
$150 Million to $500 Million	144.8	174.3	199.1	46
Under $150 Million	117.1	142.3	146.2	44

Head of Finance (Treasurer)
190 Incumbents

Size of Company (revenue)	Base Salary ($000)	Total Annual Cash Compensation ($000)	Total Direct Compensation ($000)	Total Leverage
Over $5 Billion	$180.1	$243.4	$364.6	112%
$1.5 Billion to $5 Billion	135.7	170.9	207.2	61
$500 Million to $1.5 Billion	104.4	123.7	131.6	37
$150 Million to $500 Million	100.1	124.0	143.7	61
Under $150 Million	90.6	102.6	106.2	50

Head of Accounting (Controller)
264 Incumbents

Size of Company (revenue)	Base Salary ($000)	Total Annual Cash Compensation ($000)	Total Direct Compensation ($000)	Total Leverage
Over $5 Billion	$179.8	$246.9	$389.3	125%
$1.5 Billion to $5 Billion	139.7	178.8	223.5	67
$500 Million to $1.5 Billion	108.3	132.1	141.5	37
$150 Million to $500 Million	90.2	104.7	115.9	39
Under $150 Million	73.7	83.6	83.2	23

Head of Human Resources
330 Incumbents

Size of Company (revenue)	Base Salary ($000)	Total Annual Cash Compensation ($000)	Total Direct Compensation ($000)	Total Leverage
Over $5 Billion	$208.4	$297.1	$484.7	135%
$1.5 Billion to $5 Billion	159.0	208.0	269.0	70
$500 Million to $1.5 Billion	140.6	172.2	194.0	50
$150 Million to $500 Million	107.4	126.8	146.8	41
Under $150 Million	74.5	84.9	86.4	21

Head of Research and Development
123 Incumbents

Size of Company (revenue)	Base Salary ($000)	Total Annual Cash Compensation ($000)	Total Direct Compensation ($000)	Total Leverage
Over $5 Billion	$213.2	$298.0	$500.8	139%
$1.5 Billion to $5 Billion	175.8	245.1	322.1	80
$500 Million to $1.5 Billion	151.8	186.7	207.8	49
$150 Million to $500 Million	115.1	137.4	144.5	28
Under $150 Million	97.7	115.9	119.3	29

Head of Operations
136 Incumbents

Size of Company (revenue)	Base Salary ($000)	Total Annual Cash Compensation ($000)	Total Direct Compensation ($000)	Total Leverage
Over $5 Billion	$201.1	$313.2	$491.4	144%
$1.5 Billion to $5 Billion	173.5	234.8	303.3	80
$500 Million to $1.5 Billion	158.2	194.6	225.3	56
$150 Million to $500 Million	129.2	157.9	198.2	54
Under $150 Million	105.2	123.2	125.2	40

Head of Marketing and/or Sales
378 Incumbents

Size of Company (revenue)	Base Salary ($000)	Total Annual Cash Compensation ($000)	Total Direct Compensation ($000)	Total Leverage
Over $5 Billion	$185.3	$251.8	$298.6	88%
$1.5 Billion to $5 Billion	148.4	197.5	271.3	83
$500 Million to $1.5 Billion	146.3	181.3	222.2	63
$150 Million to $500 Million	123.5	142.7	158.7	34
Under $150 Million	102.4	118.8	118.5	29

Subsidiary Head
142 Incumbents

Size of Company (revenue)	Base Salary ($000)	Total Annual Cash Compensation ($000)	Total Direct Compensation ($000)	Total Leverage
Over $5 Billion	$427.9	$741.1	$922.4	150%
$1.5 Billion to $5 Billion	379.9	649.7	988.2	170
$500 Million to $1.5 Billion	248.5	360.3	541.8	121
$150 Million to $500 Million	206.4	296.2	491.1	111
Under $150 Million	154.8	191.7	243.7	64

SOURCE: The Hay Group, 1991 "Executive Compensation Report."

These data suggest a number of conclusions, some confirming conventional wisdom, some not. For example, companies pay the chief executive officer more than any other position, even after adjusting for company size. The total direct compensation of a CEO heading a company with under $150 million annual revenue averages $268,600; the head of a subsidiary with the same revenue averages $243,700. Coincidentally, both positions have the same leverage, 64 percent.

Larger companies pay significantly more than smaller ones. For example, the CEO of a company with annual revenue of $5 billion or more is on average paid more than 10 times as much as the CEO of a company with annual revenue of less than $150 million.

What these average data mask are the large variations in pay levels within a revenue level for a particular position. The table below shows, for example, the variations for the chief executive officer.

As earlier data revealed, a significant part of the variation in total cash reflects differences in profitability at the respective companies. Nevertheless, there could be unique company-specific and other factors that could explain part of the variation. It also critical to point out that the greatest variation (4.1) is in total direct compensation, which includes a present value for current grants for long-term compensation, including options. These represent compensation *oppor tunities* and could reflect compensation policies of high-

CEO Pay Variations within Corporations with Revenue over $5 Billion

	Base Salary ($000)	Total Annual Cash Compensation ($000)	Total Direct Compensation ($000)
10th Percentile*	$ 508	$ 654	$1,099
90th Percentile*	1,140	2,046	4,519
Ratio: 90th/10th	2.2	3.1	4.1

* Indicates that 10 percent and 90 percent of the incumbents are paid less than these levels.

source: The Hay Group.

performing companies. The analysis of the pharmaceutical industry supports this hypothesis.

These executive positions are highly leveraged, which means that a large part of their compensation is at risk either in the form of annual incentive payments or in the form of long-term incentive opportunity. Generally, the larger the company, the larger the total leverage. The long-term incentive components are an opportunity that the executive may not realize unless the company achieves long-term financial goals or unless the stock price goes up.

How Rapidly Has Executive Pay Increased?

We need to examine how much pay for top management has increased relative to stock market increases, as represented by the Dow Jones Industrial Average. These data are important because they reflect relative increases in compensation levels for top management and other positions, but they also answer a question critical to our thesis. Did the executives buy their long-term incentives, particularly their stock options, in any meaningful sense of the word?

One way they could have bought these would have been if cash compensation—base salary plus bonus—increased less than the inflation rate, so that real cash compensation would have been declining at a time when the value of long-term incentive plans was increasing. If the data show smaller increases in pay relative to inflation, we conclude that the executives bought their long-term incentive plans. If, on the other hand, cash compensation increased faster than inflation at the same time long-term incentives and total direct compensation (base salary plus bonus plus the long-term value) were increasing faster than the inflation rate, we know the executives were obtaining their long-term incentive plans in addition to their cash compensation.

The following table presents data on executive pay increases over an eleven-year period, 1980–1991, comparing those increases to pay increases of lower-level employees, to the consumer price index (CPI), and to the movement of the Dow Jones Industrial Average over the same period.

This table shows that executive pay has increased dramatically over the ten-year period, 1979–1989. Executive pay increased significantly relative to that of lower-level employees and to inflation as reflected in the consumer price index. The average CEO's total direct compensation rose significantly faster than the rate of inflation, 146 percent over the period while inflation rose 80 percent.

Relative to the Dow Jones Industrial Average (DJIA), which rose 211 percent, however, these increases appear more modest. This supports the notion that the high levels of pay are justified, on the average, relative to the benefits shareholders received. For example, total direct compensation for a CEO might have increased from $500,000 to $1.2 million, a 140 percent increase, while the market value of the company might have increased from $1 billion to $3.1 billion, a 210 percent increase.

The value of long-term incentives increased dramatically

Comparing the Dow Jones Industrial Average and Executive Compensation, 1980–1991

Factor	Average Annual Increase	Total Increase
CEO Pay*		
Base Salary	8%	122%
Total Cash Compensation	9	142
Total Direct Compensation†	9	146
Entry-Level Management (Base Salary)	6	90
Inflation (CPI)	5.5	80
DJIA	11	211

* 1979–1989.
† Total cash plus present value of long-term plans.
SOURCE: The Hay Group 1991 "Executive Compensation Report;" *Securities Industry Association Yearbook, 1989.*

as well. This indicates that executives were receiving an increase in their long-term opportunity as well as an increase in their relatively fixed compensation. This conclusion is critical to our hypothesis that executives were motivated to undertake risky strategies, including acquisitions, since they had all upside opportunity and limited downside risk.

How does executive pay compare to that of athletes and entertainers? How do the top ten in each field compare?

The table below indicates that while certain CEOs earned multimillion-dollar salaries in 1991, the top entertainers and athletes did considerably better. Evander Holyfield, the boxer, earned more than the top three CEOs combined. And does Paul McCartney or George Foreman, to name two at approximately the same $15-million level, add as much economic value to the world as the CEO of Reebok?

1991 Pay Levels for Selected Occupations
($ in millions)

Rank	CEOs		Entertainers		Athletes	
1	UAL	$18	B. Cosby	$58	E. Holyfield	$60
2	Apple	17	K. Costner	50	M. Tyson	32
3	Reebok	15	O. Winfrey	42	M. Jordan	16
4	Waste Management	12	J. Carson	30	G. Foreman	15
5	U.S. Surgical	12	S. Spielberg	27	A. Senna	13
6	Walt Disney	11	M. Jackson	35	A. Prost	11
7	Warner-Lambert	8	C. Shultz	25	R. Ruddock	10
8	Fed. Nat. Mtge.	8	Madonna	24	A. Palmer	9
9	Reader's Digest	7	J. Iglesias	23	N. Mansell	9
10	Merck	7	P. McCartney	15	J. Nicklaus	9
Average		$12		$32		$18

SOURCES: *Business Week, Forbes.*

While investment banker salaries are not public knowledge in the same way that CEO, entertainer, and athlete salaries are, top-rank bankers earn between $30 million and $50 million a year, and their average cash compensation is between $15 million and $20 million.

The value our society imputes to the CEO position, as implemented by the boards of these companies, is certainly not out of line with these other occupations.

In comparing these CEO pay levels to the size of their companies, I have further evidence of the relative magnitude of these numbers. In the aggregate, sales revenue was $59 billion and profits were over $6 billion. CEO pay represents 0.2 percent and 2 percent of these values, respectively.

WHAT'S THE CEO PAY MULTIPLE?

Another controversy in CEO pay is the "rising multiple" issue. This is the multiple of CEO pay to hourly employees; if the CEO earns $500,000 and the average hourly employee earns, say, $25,000, the multiple is 20 (500,000 divided by 25,000). Critics consider this rise to be indefensible and a source of competitive disadvantage for the U.S. economy. Frederic W. Cook & Co. looked at thirty of the top Fortune 100 companies to see how the multiple had changed between 1984 and 1991. Figure 3-4 indicates that it jumped from 56 times to 113 times in those six years.

Methodological problems combined with philosophical issues change this picture, however. First, the source of the CEO data is generally "proxy" analysis, which can easily bloat CEO compensation, especially in the late 1980s when rising stock prices yielded large stock option profits. As I describe in the Appendix, we value options (and other long-term incentive programs) in the year of the grant on a *prospective* basis.

The Hay Group data in the table at the top of page 73 show a much less dramatic increase than other statistics. These

Figure 3-4
Executive Pay Differentials
Including Long Term Grant Values

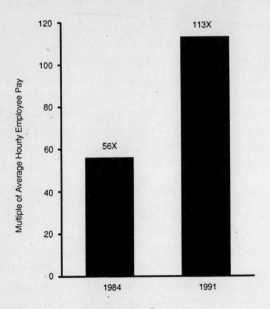

Source: Frederic W. Cook & Co., Inc., 1991
30 of Top Fortune 100 Companies.

different results stem from differences in the data source, the size of the sample, and the breadth of the companies.

While multiples have risen, they are, I believe, justified on the basis of the dramatically rising accountabilities and competitive pressures that face the CEO in 1989 versus 1979. The multiple is not rising ridiculously, and the U.S. economy remains reasonably competitive.

IS THERE ANY EXECUTIVE TURNOVER?

Do executives lose their jobs? Is executive talent brought in from outside the company, or are all CEOs internal promo-

CEO Pay Compared to Professional Pay

Year	Entry-Level Professional Pay*	CEO Pay†	Multiple
1979	$15,700	$325,000	20.7
1989	28,200	800,000	28.4

* Base salary plus bonus.
† Base salary plus bonus plus present value of long-term incentives.
SOURCE: The Hay Group data.

tions? Critics argue that most CEOs come from within the corporation, which undercuts the argument that the corporation requires high compensation levels to attract executives from outside.

To the extent that there is executive turnover, it is one indication of a relatively healthy labor market. Certainly, if there were no turnover, it would be harder to argue that corporations require high levels of compensation to attract, retain, and motivate senior executives. Further, we need to examine data on the source of CEOs. If all CEOs come from within the company, the argument about needing high and competitive levels and programs loses much of its economic fervor. The table below sheds some light on this issue. These data suggest significant executive turnover. A key question in economics is how much a particular commodity in a market must change hands for that market to be considered to be operating effectively and competitively. It is not necessary for all or even most of the units in a market to be transferred

1990 Executive Turnover

	Percent of 800 CEOs
New CEO During Past Year	20%
CEO Hired from Outside:	
Within 5 Years of 1990	11
Within 10 Years of 1990	20

SOURCE: *Forbes, 1991.*

for there to be a vigorously competitive market, but there must be some movement.

To put this into another market context: there are between 150 and 200 million automobiles in the U.S. Dealers will sell approximately 30 million cars in 1991 (15 million each of new and used)—or about 20 percent of the total. This ratio appears to reflect a market that most observers would consider reasonably competitive. Any number of additional examples, from houses to refrigerators to seats on the New York Stock Exchange, could make the point that a 20 percent turnover reflects a competitive market.

Furthermore, corporations do recruit a large number of executives from outside the company. And because they must do so, they must offer competitive and high compensation levels.

INTERNATIONAL EXECUTIVE COMPENSATION

During the early 1990s, a major international controversy arose about how high U.S. executives are paid relative to their more junior employees. Graef Crystal, for example, testified before the Senate Committee on Governmental Affairs chaired by Senator Carl Levin (D-Mich.) on May 15, 1991, at hearings entitled "The SEC and the Issue of Runaway Executive Pay." Crystal said that based on interviews he conducted for his book, *In Search of Excess,* he found that "the CEO of a major Japanese company like Sony or NEC earns around 17 times the pay of the average Japanese worker. The CEO of a major French or German company earns around 23 to 25 times the pay of the average French or German worker. The CEO of a major British company earns 33 to 35 times . . ."

Crystal looked at ten of the largest American companies and concluded that U.S. executives were paid more than 100 times what their hourly workers were paid. He concluded that this major misalignment was both unfair and a source of competitive weakness in the U.S. economy.

I disagree. The American economy is quite competitive and has been so for almost a hundred years. Joseph Nye, Jr. in *Bound to Lead: The Changing Nature of American Power* argues that the U.S. share of global output has held steady at 25 percent for virtually the entire twentieth century. The apparent decline from a 33 percent to 25 percent share from 1950 to 1980 was a temporary aberration, resulting from the rebuilding of the German and Japanese economies, which were destroyed during World War II.

Nonetheless, we want to continue (or improve) our competitiveness through all means, including how we pay our executives. While again there is room for improvement, I believe that the labor market for American executives is quite competitive and consistent with the market for executives in other Western industrialized countries and has, in fact, helped the U.S. economy remain competitive. Moreover, one can cite evidence of a consistent global labor market with reasonably similar compensation structures.

The fundamental problem with international comparisons of CEO compensation is the vastly different size of the countries and corporations being compared. The U.S. economy is twice as large as the next largest, Japan, and three to five times as large as the economies of Western Europe. The difference in economies manifests itself in the vastly different sizes of the companies in those countries. The following table shows that the U.S. has many more larger companies than other industrialized countries.

In other words, the tenth largest company in Japan was only about half as large as the tenth largest American corporation. The tenth largest company in Great Britain was only about one-fifth the size of the comparable American firm. As we've shown, executives at large corporations are paid more than executives at smaller companies. This is both logical and defensible since executives at larger companies have more responsibility and risk than do executives in smaller companies. In addition, our international database supports the notion than executives at larger companies are paid more than

**Sales Revenue of the Tenth Largest Industrial Company
($ in Billions)**

Country	Sales Revenue of Tenth Largest Company	Percent of U.S.
U.S.	$39.3	100%
Japan	20.9	53
Germany	15.1	38
France	12.7	32
United Kingdom	8.5	22
Sweden	4.5	12
Italy	2.0*	5

* Italy did not have 10 companies in the Global 500. This is an estimate.
SOURCE: *Fortune,* July 29, 1991.

executives at smaller companies in all the industrialized countries.

But these international comparisons have another major methodological problem. If I simply compare average CEO pay by country—as the previously mentioned study does— then we are comparing the CEOs of much smaller companies with those of the U.S. In addition, these studies frequently ignore the extremely generous benefit levels (for example, health insurance, pension plans, tuition reimbursement, vacation time, sick and maternity leave, paid holidays, and more) that employers pay. These benefits are extremely valuable to lower-level employees, which tends to reduce the ratios for European companies.

Assume as an illustration that an American and a European CEO each earns $1 million a year. If a lower-level American employee earns $25,000, the American CEO would have a 40 to 1 ratio ($1,000,000 divided by $25,000). If a lower-level European employee earns $40,000 because the company benefits are worth so much more, the ratio would be 25 to 1, and one can draw no accurate conclusion about American compensation relative to European. This is one reason why American multiples are higher than European.

True, American executive cash compensation is greater than European. The question is how much. These ratios make it appear that Americans earn much more, but in reality they could be very similar. In any ratio analysis, both the numerator and the denominator affect the result.

The Hay Group gathers compensation information on international compensation levels on the basis of identically sized jobs. The table below compares the total cash compensation of CEOs of $500-million companies to the pay of entry-level professionals. Note that an entry-level professional is not an hourly worker and could in fact be earning more or less than the hourly workers.

Most of the American business press seems to be using Graef S. Crystal's assertion that in Japan the CEO receives only 17 times the pay of an ordinary worker. Japanese securities regulations, however, do not require public corporations to reveal executive compensation, and they do not do so. Because Japanese law does not require disclosure the way American law does, any information about the average Jap-

International Cash Compensation and Multiples

Country	Number of Compa- nies*	Pay of Entry-Level Professional	Pay of CEO $500 Million Company†	Multiple
Japan	60	$28,400	$371,600	13.1
U.S.	530	35,300	481,000	13.6
France	243	34,300	256,600	7.5
Germany	195	49,500	767,500	15.5
United Kingdom	584	28,500	351,100	12.3
Italy	400	29,600	357,300	12.1
Average (excludes U.S.)		$34,060	$420,820	12.4

* Number of companies in entire survey in that country.
† Base plus annual incentive.
SOURCE: The Hay Group.

anese CEO's compensation has to be based on surveys, anecdotes, and gossip. Our data, among the best available,
come from our Tokyo office.

But even with our data, comparisons are very difficult.
Because the marginal tax rate in Japan is 70 to 80 percent,
Japanese executives attempt to shift compensation from their
own tax return to the corporation's. Japanese corporations
routinely give their executives benefits such as golf club
memberships, which are wildly expensive in Japan, subsi-
dized housing, transportation to the office, lavish entertainment expense accounts, foreign travel, and more.

Finally, the Japanese CEO's job is very different from the
American CEO's. In general, the Japanese executive does not
have the same responsibilities or direct involvement with the
management of the enterprise as does the American executive. One might argue therefore that the job is worth less to
the corporation.

The data in the table on page 77 are based on proprietary
figures that are comparable from country to country and
exclude benefits from both entry-level and CEO positions.
The last column shows that the U.S. multiple is not out of
line with those of other countries. This average, of course,
results primarily from the relatively low levels of cash compensation for the larger position.

Of course, these pay levels do not include income from
long-term incentive programs, especially profits from stock
options, which could be quite significant for American executives. While the American ratio (for identically sized organizations) ends up slightly higher than the multiples of
most other countries, there is no reason to believe that adding
in the long-term incentive income would distort these ratios
"obscenely" in favor of the U.S. executives.

Further, there is reason to believe that American CEOs
have significantly more accountability for strategies and financial results than their European and Japanese counterparts.
In the United Kingdom, large corporations frequently have

outside chairmen of their boards, who have significant authority. In addition, *Across the Board* magazine reported in September 1991 that ". . . power is distributed far more evenly among top executives abroad, where the CEO may be the first among equals rather than shouldering sole responsibility for the fate of millions of shareholders, employees, suppliers and customers." The international CEO's accountability, especially in Japan and Germany, is further diluted by the interlocking relationships among companies, banks, and their governments. While this arrangement has its advantages, risk—and therefore associated pay—is moved away from the top job.

Interestingly, it appears that a competitive global labor market for executives is beginning to develop. Europe and Japan are importing American-style executive compensation plans. Public (that is, "private" or non-government-owned) companies in the United Kingdom and France already make fairly extensive use of executive stock option plans; 80 to 90 percent of the eligible United Kingdom companies have such plans. There are at least two possible explanations. European executives might want to participate in an American-style gravy train; that is, they want to get rich. Or, European boards of directors want to motivate their executives to higher levels of performance, as boards have done in America. Importantly, the tax authorities in France and the United Kingdom have encouraged companies to use these stock option plans by making them even more attractive to European executives from a personal income tax perspective than the IRS has done in the U.S. In any event, European boards need to be aware of the problems with stock options that I address in this book.

THE STRUCTURE OF LONG-TERM COMPENSATION

But what are the long-term incentive programs under which executives operate? Specifically for long-term incentive plans, the piece which is intended to most directly link the interest of the shareholders with the executives, what are the different types of plans and what is wrong and right with them? The following discussion shows the types and features of various long-term incentive plans.

A long-term incentive plan is, simply, an arrangement designed to reward an individual for corporate performance over a period of more than a year. Even though the corporation may make grants and ultimately payouts yearly, what defines these plans is the longer-term performance period. Generally, the compensation value of these plans depends upon the corporation's future performance and events, as opposed to an annual incentive plan, which is based on the company's past performance and events. Thus, even though an annual incentive plan may provide for payments to be deferred in equivalent value stock units or in restricted stock, it is not a long-term incentive plan because the corporation bases the award's compensation value on performance during the past year rather than on performance over a future period of years.

Stock option plans offer an executive the right to purchase a specified number of shares of the corporation's stock at a specified price during a specified period of time. They often include alternate rights or are offered in tandem with other incentive opportunities.

In an *incentive stock option* (ISO), or qualified stock option plan, for example, the corporation gives the executive (or other employee) the right to purchase, say, 1,000 shares of the company's stock at $50 a share at any time during the next ten years. Typically the exercise price, $50, is the same as the stock's actual price on the date of the grant. It doesn't have to be that way, but it usually is.

Three years later, if the stock is trading at $80 a share, the employee could write a check for $50,000 and receive 1,000 shares of stock, which are worth $80,000. The employee's $30,000 paper profit incurs no tax liability until he or she sells the stock, and it is taxed at the capital gains rate. At many times in American tax history, capital gains rates have been materially lower than ordinary income rates, so this arrangement has benefited the employee. The drawback is that the company does not receive a tax deduction for the $30,000. Such a plan is a "tax-qualified" incentive stock option plan, or ISO.

An incentive stock option that qualifies for such favorable tax treatment under Section 422A of the Internal Revenue Code must meet certain requirements:

- The option term cannot exceed ten years.
- The option price must be at least 100 percent of fair market value at the time of the grant. If the stock is selling for $50 a share at the time of the grant, the option must be $50 or more.
- The shareholders must approve the plan with the specified requirements.
- Vesting is limited to $100,000 aggregate fair market value during any calendar year. If the stock is selling for $50 a share, the executive cannot buy more than 2,000 shares in any one year. The government has said, in effect, we're willing to give capital gains treatment on a certain amount, but don't be piggy. This limit does not affect most employees, but can constrict senior executives.

A *non-qualified stock option* (NQSO), sometimes referred to as a "non-statutory stock option," is an option that does not meet all the requirements of Section 422A of the Internal Revenue Code for incentive options. Nevertheless non-qualified options usually have a ten-year option term and are usually priced at 100 percent of market value at time of grant. There is, however, no vesting limit in any one calendar year.

In a non-qualified plan, the employee pays ordinary income tax rates at the time he or she exercises the option. Using the previous example, the employee would pay tax on the $30,000 paper profit as though it were ordinary income. So typically, employees have to sell some shares to pay the taxes. The company does get a $30,000 tax deduction, so a non-qualified stock option plan is advantageous to the company.

Since today's tax rates are basically the same for capital gains and ordinary income, most companies issue non-qualified plans so they can obtain the tax deduction, which helps their cash flow. If ordinary income tax rates increase or capital gains rates drop, the situation can change, and because of such tax rate changes, incentive stock options have gained and lost popularity two or three times in corporate history.

Stock appreciation rights (SAR) usually permit an executive to elect to receive an amount of cash or stock equal to the difference between current market value of company stock and the option price (generally subject to the corporation's administrative committee approval). This is in lieu of exercising an underlying stock option. It allows the executive to receive an amount equal to the appreciation in the stock's value without raising the money that he or she would need to exercise the stock option.

PERFORMANCE SHARE AND PERFORMANCE UNIT PLANS

A *performance share plan* (PSP) is a phantom stock asset plan that contingently grants stock units to an executive.

So-called "phantom" stock occurs in a company that does not have stock—it's privately held or a division of a larger corporation without its own shares—or, if it has stock, the owners don't wish to give any additional stock to any employees—a family company, for example, in which family members hold all the stock.

Phantom stock is a way to pretend that the company has stock so the company can use it in incentive plans for executives, so that the executives get rewarded for increasing the subsidiary's or company's economic or shareholder value. The company says, in effect, if we had stock, it would be worth "x" dollars, and that's the figure on which we're going to base our incentive plan.

Phantom stock is always inferior to real stock because no market determines its value. The company must have some methodology to estimate or some formula to develop the phantom stock's value. Nonetheless, as we'll be seeing, many companies use phantom stock in their incentive plans, and it seems to work fairly well.

These performance share grants entitle the executive to stock shares or their cash equivalent at time of payment if the company achieves predetermined financial objectives; the unit value of the stock may appreciate or decline between the initial award and the payment date. The number of units that become payable, if any, depends on the extent to which the objectives are achieved.

In such a plan, the company tells the employee in effect, you have 1,000 performance shares. Two things influence how much you ultimately receive: the company's financial performance, which will influence the number of shares, and the stock price, which will determine the value of the shares.

If, for example, the company realizes a 20 percent return on equity, the target, the executive receives 1,000 shares. If the stock is trading at $30 a share, the award is worth $30,000. If the company realizes a 25 percent return on equity, 5 percent more than target, the executive receives 1,500 shares. If the stock is trading at $40 a share, the award would be worth $60,000. If the stock, however, has dropped to $20 a share, the award would be worth $30,000.

A *performance unit plan* (PUP) contingently grants units to an executive that entitle him or her to cash payments (or their equivalent in stock) valued at the time of the award if the company achieves predetermined objectives; the unit value remains constant. A performance unit plan is similar in most respects to a performance share plan except that the value the executive receives relates to the value placed upon a share or unit at the time of grant; the value of the original units does not appreciate or decline.

For example, assume the employee has a goal of achieving a return on equity of 20 percent per year over the next three years. If the company achieves that target, the employee receives a performance unit payment of, say, $50,000. If the return on equity is above the goal, the company pays a bonus greater than $50,000; if lower than 20 percent, the bonus is smaller. Frequently, if return on equity falls below a certain threshold level, say 12 percent, there is no payment. If it goes above a certain level, say 30 percent, frequently the payouts are capped. But these are all design features and subject to board and management discussion in designing the program.

In *restricted stock plans,* the company makes awards in the form of actual shares of company stock, not the appreciation or the profit on the stock. The company transfers actual shares of stock to the employee, but they carry certain restrictions, such as prohibitions against disposition or rights of first refusal, and they may be subject to substantial risk of forfeiture. The restriction means that the employee cannot sell the stock until it vests or until the restrictions lapse.

Recently, companies have been putting in what is called time-accelerated, or performance-accelerated, restricted stock. If restrictions typically lapse in three, four, or five years, the plan would put the restrictions into effect sooner if the company attains certain higher levels of financial performance.

◆ MISCELLANEOUS STOCK EQUIVALENT PLANS

These miscellaneous stock equivalent plans include book value asset and appreciation plans, phantom stock plans, and dividend equivalent plans.

A *book value asset plan* is the same as a performance share plan, except that the value of stock units is determined according to nonmarket measurements, such as the stock's book value.

A *book value appreciation plan* is similar to a phantom stock option plan except that the payout value is determined according to the stock's book value growth or some other nonmarket evaluation.

A *phantom stock option* is a phantom stock appreciation plan that grants a number of units to an executive, each of which creates rights to a payment equal to any appreciation that occurs in the market value of a share of company stock between the date of grant and some future date, often accompanied by dividend equivalent payments. It differs from other stock incentive plans in that the company transfers no stock to a participating executive. Although companies usually use stock units to determine the payment amount an executive may receive, the company transfers no equity interest to the executive, issues no stock certificates, and pays no dividends. The executive receives a simulation of stock ownership. Since a phantom stock option plan is an appreciation plan, the executive never receives the initial value of the units or shares granted, but rather receives the future appreciation or income (dividend equivalents) attributable to those units.

A *dividend equivalent plan* is a phantom stock income plan that grants a number of units to an executive, each of which creates rights to a payment equal to any dividends paid on a share of the company's stock. Dividend equivalent plans are similar in format and in most characteristics to phantom stock option plans, except that they limit payment to dividend equivalents and do not include any appreciation, as do phantom stock option plans.

In most instances, companies connect dividend equivalent payment plans with another long-term plan.

LONG-TERM INCENTIVE PLAN DESIGN

What percentage of companies actually employ these various plans? One hundred and thirty-nine organizations supplied data to the 1991 Hay Group "Executive Compensation Report—Industrial Management" covering about 337 distinct long-term incentive plans. The following discussion analyzes those data for stock option (that is, incentive stock options, non-qualified stock options, and stock appreciation rights), restricted stock, performance share, performance unit, and phantom stock plans.

Stock option plans continue to be the most prevalent; 82 percent of the companies with long-term incentive plans reported having at least one. Of the companies with option plans, most use non-qualified stock options (86 percent), followed by incentive stock options (57 percent) and stock appreciation rights (42 percent). As Figure 3-5 illustrates, a significant portion of the organizations in our survey also use equity-based plans (restricted stock, performance share or unit, or phantom stock plans in which the executive obtains equity value as well as appreciation value).

Of the organizations supplying long-term incentive plan data, 40 percent report restricted stock plans, 26 percent performance units, 24 percent performance shares, and 18 percent phantom or miscellaneous plans.

A large portion of plans, particularly performance share, restricted stock and non-qualified stock options, were adopted in 1990, as Figure 3-5 illustrates. Typically, a company added the performance share or restricted stock plan to existing stock option plans—rarely did they stand alone or pair with a non-option plan. In fact, over two-thirds of the surveyed companies reported more than one long-term incentive plan, with some (4 percent) reporting as many as six, as Figure 3-6 illustrates.

Many of these plans are in tandem with another (primarily options), but the trend appears to be moving solidly toward multiple plans.

Figure 3-7 identifies the most prevalent combinations. Some 37 percent of the companies in the Executive Compensation Report database, for example, have stock options

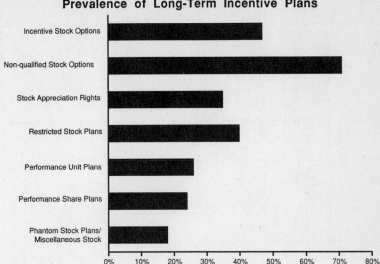

Figure 3-5
Prevalence of Long-Term Incentive Plans

Source:1991 The Hay Group "Executive Compensation Report."

with restricted stock while 22 percent have stock options with performance shares.

Figure 3-6 indicates the popularity of various plans companies adopted in 1990. For example, stock option plans (including incentive stock options, non-qualified stock options, and stock appreciation rights) were 28 percent of the total, while performance plans (including both unit and share plans) accounted for 32 percent. The figures add to 84 percent; the remaining 16 percent had other programs or didn't specify the new programs.

Although the prevalence of long-term incentive plans is growing overall, the percentage of companies awarding grants (illustrated in the table on page 89) in any given year depends on whether the company designs the plan (or plans)

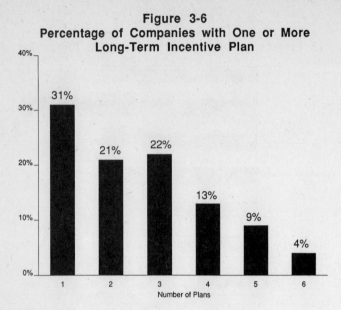

Figure 3-6
Percentage of Companies with One or More Long-Term Incentive Plan

Source:1991 The Hay Group "Executive Compensation Report."

to award grants annually or based on some other time period. The table reveals that many plans are not designed for annual awards; while nearly three out of four non-qualified stock option plans are designed for annual awards, only five restricted stock plans are so designed. As I noted earlier, a significant portion of the surveyed companies offer two or more plans, and they will often stagger their grant cycles so that an executive actually receives an award annually even if the individual plans do not make grants every year.

The vast majority of companies indicated that they do *not* provide separate plans for separate operating units. The only notable exception was performance unit plans; 11 percent of the companies reporting indicated they did have separate plans for operating units.

Most companies use a formula to allocate the number of shares, as the table at the bottom of page 90 illustrates. There

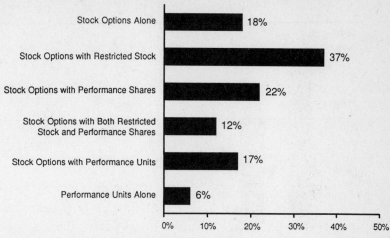

Figure 3-7
Combinations of Long-Term Incentive Plans

Source:1991 The Hay Group "Executive Compensation Report."

appears to be more formula usage with performance-based plans (about 80 percent of the plans are formula-driven) than with stock option–based plans (60 percent). Differences also exist between these two types of plans with respect to whether the formula is based on salary level or executive title. Stock option plans are twice as likely to use salary levels as a basis for allocating shares, while the performance-based plans are evenly split between salary levels and title. In other words, 53 percent of the companies offering incentive stock

Percentage of Adoptions of Plans in 1990

	STOCK OPTIONS			PERFORMANCE		
ISO	NQSO	SAR	Restricted Stock	Units	Shares	Phantom Stock
9%	13%	6%	16%	8%	24%	8%

SOURCE: 1991 Hay Group "Executive Compensation Report."

Percentage of Companies with Plans and Grants

| | STOCK OPTIONS | | | | PERFORMANCE | | |
	ISO	NQSO	SAR	Restricted Stock	Units	Shares	Phantom Stock
Percentage of Companies with Annual Grant	44	73	58	38	50	59	56
Percentage of Companies with 1990 Grants	45	86	63	62	67	65	72

SOURCE: 1991 Hay Group "Executive Compensation Report."

options use an allocation formula to do so. The figures add to more than 100 percent because companies offer more than one program.

Corporations typically make grants using fair market value at the time of the grant to determine the award's value. The table at the top of page 91 presents those values as a percentage of salary.

The figures indicate that among chief executive officers who received incentive stock options, the median grant was 95 percent of their salaries. Among other executives, the comparable median grant was 50 percent.

Percentage of Companies Using a Formula to Allocate Shares

| | STOCK OPTIONS | | | | PERFORMANCE | | |
	ISO	NQSO	SAR	Restricted Stock	Units	Shares	Phantom Stock
Percentage Using Allocation Formula	53	67	63	59	83	77	48

SOURCE: 1991 Hay Group "Executive Compensation Report."

Median Grant Size as a Percentage of Salary

| | STOCK OPTIONS | | | | PERFORMANCE | | |
	ISO	NQSO	SAR	Restricted Stock	Units	Shares	Phantom Stock
CEOs	95%	100%	100%	65%	60%	75%	*
Other Executives	50	50	65	40	45	50	*

* Insufficient data.

SOURCE: 1991 Hay Group "Executive Compensation Report."

When a corporation offers multiple plans, it usually grants restricted stock and performance shares in addition to stock option plans rather than issued in tandem, which in the language of executive compensation usually means one *or* the other—stock options *or* performance units—and the executive can receive the profits from whichever has the greater value. Most companies today use additive plans, where the executive does receive both.

Stock appreciation rights are usually found in tandem with incentive stock options or non-qualified stock options or both, although over a third of the plans in the survey were reported as freestanding. The table below illustrates the percentage of plans that have additive versus tandem features. In nearly all cases (80 percent for stock options and 100 percent for other plans), the organization rather than the executive chooses the grant type when multiple plans exist.

Multiple Plans Are Additive or in Tandem

| | STOCK OPTIONS | | | | PERFORMANCE | | |
	ISO	NQSO	SAR	Restricted Stock	Units	Shares	Phantom Stock
Additive	77%	70%	36%	88%	70%	83%	83%
Tandem	23	30	64	12	30	17	17

SOURCE: 1991 Hay Group "Executive Compensation Report."

The vast majority of vesting provisions are based on continued employment; 90 percent of the incentive stock option plans and 97 percent of the stock appreciation rights plans have this provision. In other words, the executive receives the grant only after remaining with the company for a specified time, although nearly a third of the performance share plans have provisions that make vesting also contingent upon the corporation's financial performance. This is a major improvement over purely time-based vesting because employees are doubly motivated to attain their financial targets. They get a bigger payout, and they get it more quickly. The table on page 93 illustrates these vesting and timing provisions.

As the table indicates, most plans vest in full rather than in installments, although about half the restricted stock plans vest in installments, half in full. Option plans characteristically vest in full after one year, while the vesting period for non-option plans coincides with the plan cycles (typically three years, but four-year or five-year plans are also common).

Other Incentive Plan Characteristics

Survey respondents that have option plans do not typically provide financial assistance with their long-term incentive awards; this assistance occasionally includes loans or tax offset bonuses. About half the companies responding did indicate that an executive could satisfy the tax liability by share withholding.

To exercise options, all plans allow cash as the form of payment; about two-thirds allow the use of company stock, and one-third allow broker's notice. Figure 3-8 shows the typical combinations of payment forms reported for the plans in this survey.

Only 4 percent of the plans canceled and regranted in the last year. A company will cancel and regrant because the stock options issued at, say, $30 a share are currently trading

Vesting Provisions and Timing

| | STOCK OPTIONS | | | | PERFORMANCE | | |
	ISO	NQSO	SAR	Restricted Stock	Units	Shares	Phantom Stock
Based on Continued Employment	90%	88%	97%	88%	83%	68%	90%
Contingent upon Performance	10	12	3	12	NA	32	10
Award vests: In full	51	61	57	53	70	75	60
In Installments	49	39	43	47	30	25	40
Typical Number of Installments	3	3	3	3 or 5	3	2–4	*
Vesting Typically Begins After (Number of Years)	1	1	1	1 (installment) 3 (full)	1 (installment) 3 (full)	1 (installment) 3 (full)	

* Insufficient data.
SOURCE: 1991 Hay Group "Executive Compensation Report."

for $25; the options are, in option language, "under water." This is a problem for companies because the options no longer hold any appeal to the employee. So some companies, 4 percent in 1991, canceled the old option and reissued a new

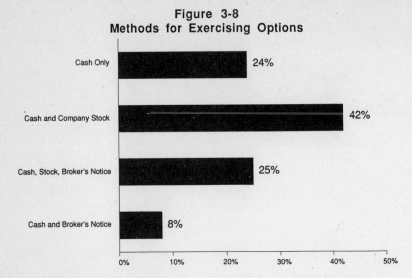

Figure 3-8
Methods for Exercising Options

Source:1991 The Hay Group "Executive Compensation Report'."

one at current market value. The best-known example of this practice is Apple Computer, which has canceled and regranted a number of times. Shareholders generally frown on these cancel and reissue plans.

How do executives exercise their stock options? And what forms of payment did they use?

For restricted stock, performance units, and performance shares, only about 4 percent of the plans required executives to invest their own funds to receive grants, according to the Hay Group study.

Most plans pay out at the end of the plan cycle; only 18 percent of the restricted stock plans, 13 percent of the performance unit plans, and 4 percent of the performance share plans permit the recipient to defer payment. Fewer than 10 percent of the deferral features are optional.

Performance-based plans typically use corporate performance, rather than division or subsidiary performance, as a basis for determining earnouts. Most companies cited earnings per share or return on equity as the criterion they use to evaluate executive performance. Two out of three of these plans state performance in absolute terms, that is, the executives must obtain a specific return on equity to obtain their performance units, or whatever.

The other alternative is a relative measure. Performance is measured relative to, say, ten other competitors. The company has to outperform their average performance, whether up or down, for the executives to obtain their performance units, or whatever. This arrangement protects the shareholders on the upside in high-performing years, because if industry performance goes up dramatically and the company does not perform as well, it does not pay an incentive.

On the downside, if the company's performance goes down, but not as much as its competitors', it pays a performance bonus anyway. I recommend adding an absolute measure such as return on equity or return on assets to the relative return on equity or return on assets. The matrix in Figure 3-9 indicates four possible outcomes. If the company's return on assets is both above target and above competition, the executive receives the maximum incentive payout. If the performance is below target but above the competition, or below the competition but above the target, the company pays the approximate target incentive payout.

These data permit several conclusions:

1. Stock options are the most common form of long-term incentive plan.
2. There is a vast array of plans with countless individual features.
3. Many companies have more than one long-term incentive plan.
4. Very few of these plans create a balance in the risk profiles between shareholders and executives.

Figure 3-9
Matrix of Different Performance Scenarios
Based on Relative Plus Absolute Return on Assets (ROA)

		Absolute ROA	
		Below Target	Above Target
Relative ROA	Above Competition	Approximate Target Incentive Payout	Maximum Incentive Payout
	Below Competition	Minimum Incentive Payout	Approximate Target Incentive Payout

The great success of many American corporations must be in part reflective of their compensation plan for their key executives. I maintain that executives found stock options to be highly motivating, but that they were flawed in their design. The primary manifestation of that flaw was their role in takeovers, as the next chapter describes.

CHAPTER 4

Executive Compensation as a Cause of Takeovers

*The failure of . . . management to put
significant equity into their own deals has
dramatically increased the probability that deals
are overpriced.*

—Michael Jensen

The Time Warner merger, consummated in January 1990, was again in the news in the summer of 1991. This time, Time Warner was trying an equity-for-debt swap using some fancy investment banking mechanisms, essentially a shareholder rights offering, common in the United Kingdom, with a floating (upward) stock price. The deal sounded like this: If the shareholders did not exercise their rights to buy the new offering, the shares would be diluted; if they did exercise their rights, they did not know the price of the shares they would be buying.

If that's unclear, it's because no one in the universe understood the arrangement. I heard experienced investment bankers say that this was the most complicated deal they had ever seen. Under pressure from the Securities and Exchange Commission and the shareholders, combined with negative publicity, Time Warner changed the deal to a $2.8 billion standard equity offering, one of the largest in history. People observed that this was the second time in two years the Time shareholders received a raw deal. The first time was 1990, when the Time Inc. board of directors rejected a $200-per-share offer from Paramount to buy Time in favor of their own acquisition of Warner Communications, an acquisition that required enormous debt and, as one consequence, the 1991 deal.

The board of directors approved the Warner acquisition, and a ruling by the Delaware courts (where Time was incorporated) supported it. The court's logic was that the board knew what was best for the shareholders, and that the board truly believed a Time Warner merger would yield synergies and beneficial economics. The Time Inc. management argued that such benefits would ultimately yield a stock price equivalent to $400 in today's terms (versus the $200 Paramount offer and the $127 price prior to the offer).

While the jury is still out on Time Warner's ultimate value, the stock price two years after the merger is below $100. On a present value basis, it will be extremely difficult for the former Time Inc. shareholders to ever recover their losses.

WERE MANAGEMENT'S INTERESTS ALIGNED WITH THE SHAREHOLDERS'?

The key question remains: Why did the Time Inc. board reject the Paramount bid on management's clear recommendation? The synergy and strategy argument may have some merit. But what were management's economic interests? Were they aligned with those of the shareholders? While the Time Inc. management might have rejected the Paramount bid under any circumstances, analysis after the fact shows that it may have been more advantageous economically for the managers to protect their current and future compensation programs than to be "cashed out" in a Paramount purchase.

As a general rule, it is never advisable to have management making critical or strategic decisions that run counter to the owners' economic interests. Forced to choose between their own interests and the shareholders', shareholders may suffer. Consider the figures in the table below.

Richard Munroe's total cash compensation in 1988 was over $1.5 million; the company had granted him over 26,000 stock options a year, 91,000 of which he had not yet exercised.

Using the $200-per-share offer, I compared the incremental value of the stock Munroe and Nicholas owned to the present value of their annual compensation. The incremental value of the stock was equal to the total number of shares they owned times $73, the difference between the $200-per-share offer and the price of the stock at the time.

To obtain the present value of their annual compensation I made several assumptions: that they would hold the same jobs until retirement (seven years for Munroe; sixteen years for Nicholas); a 9 percent discount rate (risk-free rate of return); that cash compensation would increase at 9 percent a year (based on the 1980–1990 average increase for all executives); and that Time Inc. would grant options each year equal to the average of the 1986–1989 grants, valued at the takeover price, which would also increase 9 percent a year.

While one might dispute these individual assumptions, and therefore the magnitude of the outcome, the results them-

Where Time Inc.'s CEO and President Stood in 1989

Position	Name	1988 Total Cash Compensation	1986–1989 Average Annual Options Granted	Total Stock Owned	Total Stock Options
CEO	R. Munroe	$1,525,303	26,400	117,860	91,825
President	N. Nicholas	$1,299,532	18,750	51,454	67,821

SOURCE: 1989 Time Inc. proxy statement.

Alternative Scenarios for the Time Inc. CEO and President

	Paramount Takeover Scenario: Present Value of Stock Appreciation at Takeover Price	Status Quo Scenario: Present Value of Annual Compensation
Munroe	$15,307,000	$24,167,000
Nicholas	8,707,000	42,692,000

selves would not be very different. My calculations are shown in the table above.

In other words, if Paramount had taken over Time Inc., Munroe would have walked away with more than $15 million, a considerable sum of money. In rejecting the offer and buying Warner, however, he stood to make considerably more. In fact, he retired from Time Inc. at the time of the acquisition. Significantly, Nicholas became the co-CEO with Steve Ross*. The Time Inc. shareholders not only lost the $200 per share from Paramount, they've watched their stock sink, at this writing, to the $80 range, losing $80 to $120 per share based on the 1989–1990 trading range.

Based on this analysis, it is apparent that these key decision makers' economic interests were not the same as the shareholders'. The survival of Time Inc. in a similar corporate form yielded greater economic value to Munroe and Nicholas than a change in control. Munroe and Nicholas may have truly believed that the shareholders were better off with the Warner acquisition than by being purchased by Paramount; nevertheless, shareholders could have been more confident their interests were being fairly represented had these executives' interests been identical to theirs. If the CEO and president gained or lost as much or as little as the outside shareholders, the owners could be somewhat more confident the executives were representing their interests fairly.

As I discussed in Chapter 1, the results for the Warner

---

* N. Nicholas has subsequently left Time Warner.

Communications shareholders were very different than those for the Time Inc. shareholders. The Warner stockholders did extremely well in this transaction, obtaining $14 billion in total, a 50 percent premium over the price at which the stock was trading prior to the offer. Steven Ross, the Warner CEO, did extraordinarily well. He owned 830,696 shares, for which Time paid $193 million, and, interestingly, he held no options. Ross has received extensive bad publicity for his personal compensation levels (and even his lifestyle); Graef Crystal has called him "the Prince of Pay."

It is ironic and a sad comment on the state of American capitalism that Ross gets criticized while earning his shareholders billions, whereas the Time executives escaped media and public scrutiny. Perhaps they deserve more attention because their shareholders did not do as well as Ross's. Ross's interests and those of his shareholders were directly linked. Was it coincidental that he acted in their (and his) best interests? Naturally, the long-run prospects for Time Warner shareholders are uncertain, although with Ross at the helm, their future could be excellent.

Michael R. Klein, a lawyer, wrote in the winter 1990 issue of *Directors & Boards,* "The facts of this case—and there's little dispute about it—suggest that Time management negotiated this transaction with Warner quite clearly with their own succession in mind and their own perquisites and salary at the forefront."

WHO BENEFITS FROM A TAKEOVER?

Low levels of executive stock ownership combined with risk-free long-term incentive plans played a major role in the merger wave that occurred during the late 1980s. As Mark Kroll, Susan Simmons, and Peter Wright pointed out not long ago in the *Journal of Business Research:* "If . . . firm size significantly influences CEO rewards, then significant changes in firm size achieved through acquisition should pay handsome dividends for the CEO. . . . This rather appealing logic may explain a large part of the continuing corporate interest in acquisition in spite of some significant evidence that suggests that such activity affords shareholders few, if any, benefits."

While the business and academic literature contain many explanations for takeovers, the essential questions are: Who benefits from a takeover, and why do takeovers occur?

In examining the literature and logic of the takeover craze, some broad basic themes are apparent.

1. The acquired company shareholders usually benefit significantly, while the acquiring company shareholders do not benefit at all. Indeed, the shareholders from the buying company frequently lose significant value. Adding the values for the two companies together usually does yield a slight positive economic gain.

2. The executives and the boards of the acquiring company generally argue they need to make the acquisition to increase profitability. These profits, they say, will occur through cost cutting, improved distribution, and other advantages. More often than not, these forecasted benefits do not fully materialize, primarily because the acquiring company paid too much for the target.

3. Large corporations, as the last chapter showed, pay their senior executives more than smaller companies pay for comparable jobs. Diversified firms—conglomerates—pay better than companies with a single line of business. And while more profitable companies pay better than less profitable ones, size and diversification play major roles in animating management to make acquisitions.

To clarify the role of executive pay in takeovers, it is essential to distinguish between different types of acquisitions, which can be characterized or "typed" a number of ways. These include:

Friendly versus unfriendly.

Horizontal (same industry) versus vertical (vendor/customer).

Related industry versus conglomerate.

Merger versus takeover.

Stock versus cash (or other securities).

Purchase of stock versus purchase of assets.

Purchase versus pooling, or a swap of stock, which can be advantageous from accounting and tax perspectives.

CORPORATE BUYERS AND FINANCIAL TAKEOVER SPECIALISTS

No distinction is more important than the motivation and nature of the acquirer. The buyer's *nature* can predict the ultimate price paid, the extent of the cost reductions, and the implementation of synergies. The buyer's nature, in short, foreshadows the likelihood of an acquisition's success or failure.

Before I go further, I should distinguish the two types of buyers of other companies. The general business public tends to lump all takeover activity together. This makes it difficult to identify takeover motivation or to measure the different outcomes, so it is critical to distinguish between types—the "financial" buyers ("raiders," "takeover artists," "takeover specialists") and the "corporate" or "strategic" buyers (that is, one company buying another). For clarity and consistency's sake, and with no disparaging intent, I will call the former "financial takeover specialists" and the latter "corporate buyers."

Corporate buyers are one organization, almost always publicly traded and generally with widely dispersed and significant institutional ownership. Management stock ownership tends to be fairly low, typically less than 5 percent. How much stock the managers own will become the essential variable for predicting the likelihood of an acquisition's success. An example is the Time Warner acquisition.

A financial takeover specialist is typically a financial organization that invests in operating companies. It tends to be fairly narrowly owned, with the principals making the investment decisions, even if a large part of the invested capital belongs to others. Examples include Kohlberg, Kravis, Roberts and Mesa Partners. The table on page 105 distinguishes further between these two types of buyers.

Based on these attributes, it is no surprise that the financial takeover specialists tend to be much more successful in their acquisitions than are corporate buyers. Financial economists believe that financial takeover specialists disciplined the use of free cash flow by corporations during the late 1980s. They did so by either taking over or by threatening to take over those organizations that wasted their free cash flow, the cash generated in excess of the amount the corporation needed to maintain the current level of invested capital.

In a study of sixty-two hostile takeovers, Sanjai Bhagat and his associates found that around one-third of the hostile takeovers they studied were attempted by financial takeover specialists, the rest by another corporation. These authors speculate that the returns to the financial takeover specialists were higher than the returns to the corporate buyers.

One 1985 study in the *Journal of Financial Economics* showed that in addition to achieving superior returns for themselves, financial takeover specialists achieved superior returns for all the target company's shareholders and, further, generally improved the target company's management.

Takeovers by financial takeover specialists dropped dramatically in the early 1990s. This occurred for a number of reasons: the collapse of junk bonds, state anti-takeover legislation, and the virtual universal use of poison pills. But while the financial takeover specialists may not return in force, unless the executive compensation programs at major corporations change significantly, it is highly likely that

How Financial Takeover Specialists Differ from Corporate Buyers

Attribute	Corporate Buyer	Financial Takeover Specialist
1. Buyer's Ownership Status	Public	Generally private
2. Target Company's Attributes	Same industry or diversification; poor or strong performer	Always diversifies; high cash flow/low growth
3. Shares of Buying Company Owned by Decision Makers	Small	Large
4. Compensation of Decision Makers	Generally based on operating results, including size of company	Based heavily or solely on asset appreciation
5. Assumes Operating Responsibility for Target	Generally yes	Generally no
6. Post-acquisition Strategy	Pursues synergies; modest cost cutting	Aggressive cost cutting
7. Corporate Staff of Buyer	Large	Small
8. Purchase Mechanism	Pooling (stock) or cash; some leverage	Highly leveraged; hybrid securities plus cash

value-reducing corporate acquisitions will explode over the next few years.

This is a key point. The financial takeover specialists acted as an external discipline on management that kept many executives more conservative in terms of their strategies and cash flow management than they might otherwise have been.

They were afraid of being taken over or they were actually taken over. Without the financial takeover specialists on the scene, corporate managers lose a source of potential (or actual) discipline. Unless long-term incentive plans change, therefore, unsuccessful acquisitions will increase dramatically.

I focus on corporate buyers, since there are so many more of them than financial takeover specialists, but, more to the point, *they are the ones who are influenced by their compensation programs.*

WHY THE TAKEOVER CRAZE OCCURRED

Our corporations have made our national economy rich and strong. The effective management of those corporations is essential to the nation's future prosperity. Carefully examining the policies that guide those companies can increase the probability of success.

Michael Jensen wrote in the *Harvard Business Review* in 1989 that the American corporation has been eclipsed. His primary point was that low growth/high cash flow companies (oil, chemicals, consumer products, tobacco, and others) have a legal structure that is inconsistent with the interests of their owners, the public shareholders. These companies have too little debt and too much equity, and their key executives hold too few shares of the company's stock.

Jensen argued that the lack of debt creates huge amounts of free cash flow, which should be paid to shareholders (through stock repurchase or special dividends). The shareholders, after all, enjoy higher return opportunities than do the companies. Many companies did not give this free cash flow to shareholders; rather, they tended to spend it on investment projects or acquisitions that did not create shareholder value. We'll be discussing management motivation to undertake these projects, but for now it's enough to observe there were clear advantages for managers to keep the cash flow under their control. These combined to create a situation where the interests of management—as at Time Inc.—were not necessarily those of the owners.

While many industries and companies are addressing this situation, Jensen argued that many more industries should follow suit. While I agree with the argument's main thrust, I agree with others—for example, Alfred Rappaport—who argue that with some fairly dramatic restructuring, the corporate form cannot only be saved but can be revitalized. This would require addressing the symptoms outlined above: Dramatically increase management's stock ownership and financially restructure to create more discipline over free cash flow. Financial restructuring may require increased debt, less perhaps than the insupportable levels at some companies, but more than American corporations have historically tolerated. (Japanese companies typically have much higher debt levels than do American companies.)

Within the context of these themes, three broad arguments explain the corporate buyer takeover craze.

The profitability/shareholder value-creation argument. This position holds that the acquiring company is searching for ways to release the economic value hidden within the target company. This value, as we'll show, has many sources. In general, the corporate buyers successfully release a great deal of value, but it is generally insufficient to cover the premium they pay for the target. Both corporate buyers and financial takeover specialists state "releasing value" as a primary goal in making an acquisition. But it appears the corporate buyers are not as skilled at releasing that value (either because they pay too much, because they do not cut costs as sharply, because they are not as proficient at asset sales, or for all these reasons and more) as are the financial takeover specialists (Kohlberg, Kravis, Roberts; Clayton & Dubilier; and others).

The capital markets argument. This position has two basic components. First, the availability of cheap, readily available financing, in the form of junk bonds, bank financing, bridge loans from investment banks, and institutional funds in general (pension funds and other insurance funds), meant enormous amounts of capital were searching for above-average rates of return. Second, investment bankers were driven by huge fees to search for the incremental deal, whether it made economic sense or not.

First Boston and Citicorp, for example, earned $600 million in fees to help Robert Campeau buy Allied Stores, although the man had a spotty career as a shopping center, apartment, and office building developer, no experience as a retailer, and was, according to John Rothchild (in *Going for Broke*), cash poor. Although Campeau could not make the downpayment for his Allied Stores purchase, First Boston and Citicorp were willing to help him then buy Federated Stores, a transaction that generated $200 million in fees for First Boston—more than Federated earned in a year. Six months after that transaction, Campeau went bankrupt.

The managerial objectives argument. This states that managers have their own reasons to pursue acquisitions despite the fact that the spoils are as likely to destroy shareholder value as to create it. My basic point—that managers own too little stock or have too many stock options (or both) to truly act in the interests of all of shareholders—falls squarely under this argument, and I believe this is one of the primary motivations for the takeover craze. It is also a point the business media completely missed.

In examining takeovers, the media in fact have focused primarily on how greedy the executives were from two perspectives. One perspective missed the essential point, and the other was 180 degrees in the wrong direction.

Companies where executive stock ownership is relatively low usually introduce corporate takeover defense mechanisms such as golden parachutes (special large severance payments to executives who lose their jobs as a result of having their company taken over), poison pills, and the like. While the media have given these defenses enormous attention, they seldom acknowledge that the companies need these plans to ensure that their executives will evaluate a takeover proposal fairly, taking in both shareholder and management interests.

Second, the media focused on the large payouts to executives in takeovers. But these payouts can be criticized only when the shareholders do not earn a significant premium over the stock's price prior to the takeover offer. Ross Johnson, CEO of R. J. Reynolds, and Charles Exley of NCR personally made millions of dollars when their companies were taken over and received enormous negative publicity. The press did not trumpet that their shareholders received $25 billion and $7 billion dollars, respectively, huge premiums over the pre-takeover value. That appears to be superior to a situation where the executives do not get rich (or get rich through non-stock programs such as a golden parachute, for example) and the shareholders do not enjoy a premium for their stock.

Low executive stock ownership creates a potential problem on both sides of the takeover equation. Executives who own little stock will resist being taken over because their own economic interests may be better served by continuing their employment contracts in the existing corporate form. This may have been the case at Time Inc. As Michael Jensen pointed out in the *Journal of Economic Perspectives,* a golden parachute allows the executive to evaluate a takeover offer for its benefits to the shareholders solely, removing the executive's economic loss from the decision. Jensen points out that the *announcement* of a new golden parachute plan has tended to raise the company's stock price, as the market perceives a higher likelihood of a takeover (and takeover premium) since executives will not resist the takeover. But while parachutes may benefit the shareholders of target companies, they do not solve the problem of the executives with low stock ownership making bad acquisitions. It is ironic that parachutes receive bad publicity, despite their apparent benefit to shareholders. Nevertheless, high executive stock ownership addresses both problems, and I consider it a superior approach.

If executive compensation plans had been different there would have been fewer, or certainly better, acquisitions. This argument centers around the concept of "agency theory," which states that managers are the agents of the shareholders, but their interests are not always aligned. This argument may also partially explain why the financial takeover specialists did so much better in their acquisitions than did the corporate buyers. The decision makers at the financial takeover firms own the companies; the money they risk includes their own.

WHY DO TAKEOVERS OCCUR?

Before I explore the specific role that executive compensation played in the "merger mania" that occurred during the 1980s, it is important, informative, and interesting to examine the other reasons for American takeovers.

Acquiring companies take over other companies ostensibly to increase the parent company's value. Even if managerial reasons for takeovers exist (reasons separate and distinct from the shareholder reasons—for example, to increase the company's size so the managers may increase their compensation and their "power" in the executive community), executives will try to maximize shareholder value even as they try to meet their own managerial objectives.

But why do the acquiring company's executives think they can create value for their shareholders by managing the acquired company so much better than the former managers? Obviously, they think that they can squeeze out more profit or a greater cash flow than the old management could. This increased profitability could come from one or more sources.

1. Increased market share from horizontal integration— that is, a company buying one of its competitors. This could explain mergers in damaged industries. Research data sup-

port this thesis, showing that acquired companies have very low market-to-book value ratios. It also implies that the relaxed antitrust environment created during the Reagan presidency may have played a significant role in the takeover craze.

2. Significant cost savings from the combined companies, especially in the form of employee layoffs—cutting the redundant staff. In 1991, the Chemical Bank–Manufacturers Hanover merger fell into this camp.

3. "Deconglomeritization." The acquiring company creates value by selling assets to reduce debt or to allow management to focus its attention on the remaining businesses.

4. Meaningful tax advantages. These often come in the form of net operating losses the acquiring company can carry forward (called NOLs in merger and acquisition talk).

5. Cutbacks in research and development or in investments. These could help pay for the acquisition, although studies on R&D have shown that increasing R&D increases market valuation. So unless the R&D or the investments being made are destroying value (as some authors argue has occurred in the petroleum industry), cutting R&D will not be a long-term source of value for the acquiring company. Bio-technology firms—Biogen, for one—are examples of companies that report losses and yet, based on a future return on today's R&D, the stock market values them highly.

Since the acquired company's shareholders benefit a great deal and the acquiring shareholders lose just a little, takeovers represent major improvements in economic efficiency. One estimate by Jensen (in "Corporate Control and the Politics of Finance") is that shareholder value increased $650 billion from 1976 to 1990 (in 1990 dollars).

One motivation to acquire is strategic positioning, buying a company with a superior distribution system or a complementary product line. Examples in the consumer products and pharmaceutical industry include Bristol-Myers and

Squibb; examples in financial services and investment banking include American Express and Shearson Lehman. Other acquisitions reflect strategic error—making an acquisition or investment that does increase earnings, but which generates returns below the cost of capital and thereby erodes and eventually destroys shareholder value.

The five reasons above partially explain why corporations buy other companies. Since most, if not all, of the benefit accrues to the *acquired* company, the question still remains: Why do companies make acquisitions?

Jensen has shown (in the *Journal of Economic Perspectives,* Winter 1988) a clear pattern in the types of companies and industries in which takeovers occur. He argues that industries with high cash flow and relatively low growth opportunities are prime targets. Even industries, such as banking, that do not have particularly high cash flows benefit from takeover activity as a form of retrenchment that reduces the industry's excess capacity.

"This slow growth has increased takeover activity because takeovers play an important role in facilitating exit from an industry or activity," Jensen writes. "Major changes in energy markets, for example, have required a radical restructuring and retrenchment in that industry, and takeovers have played an important role in accomplishing these changes; oil and gas rank first in takeover activity, with twice their proportionate share of total activity." The following table, in which industries are ranked by takeover activity, compares activity to total corporate market value. While mining and minerals companies, for example, accounted for 4.4 percent of total takeover activity, the acquisitions in that industry accounted for only 1.5 percent of total corporate market value.

If incumbent management does not respond aggressively to external changes, then the market for corporate control does it for them. As the table shows, banking is very high in merger activity. This industry, as with others on the list, has

Takeover Activity Compared to Market Value

Industry Classification of Seller	Percent of Total Take-over Activity	Percent of Total Corporate Market Value
Oil and gas	26.3%	13.5%
Banking and finance	8.8	6.4
Insurance	5.9	2.9
Food processing	4.6	4.4
Mining and minerals	4.4	1.5
Conglomerate	4.4	3.2
Retail	3.6	5.2
Transportation	2.4	2.7
Leisure and entertainment	2.3	0.9
Broadcasting	2.3	0.7
Other	39.4	58.5

SOURCE: *Journal of Economic Perspectives,* Winter 1988.

been experiencing deregulation and other forms of heightened global competitiveness; mergers or takeovers are the market's healthy response to this externally created excess capacity, the need for economies of scale, and other forms of revenue enhancement or cost cutting.

When a corporation makes an acquisition, the capital available to its industry is reduced since the shareholders of the target company receive the cash proceeds directly. Jensen argues that while these acquisitions may not have high returns for the corporate buyer, they may well be superior for the buying company's shareholders since even these acquisitions are better than some other form of internal investment. "Because the bidding firms are using funds that would otherwise have been spent on low- or negative-return projects," he wrote in the *Journal of Economic Perspectives* (Winter 1988), "the opportunity cost of the funds is lower than their cost of capital. As a result, they will tend to overpay for the acquisition and thereby transfer some, if not all, of the gains to the target firm's shareholders."

Examples of industries facing these issues include oil, food, tobacco, forest products, and broadcasting, all industries where the current performance is quite high both in profit and cash flow but the opportunities for growth are quite limited, whether due to licensing issues (broadcasting) or health reasons (tobacco).

This theory predicts that two very different types of companies will be takeover targets: poor performers, where the acquiring company has an opportunity to improve performance; and companies with a strong cash flow, where the acquiring company can benefit from having money to pay off debt. Jensen concludes that his "free cash flow" takeover theory goes a long way to explain why so many companies have been taken over.

"GOOD" VERSUS "BAD" ACQUISITIONS

One can, and must, categorize corporate strategies, including investment and acquisition strategies, as "good" or "bad." While executives at the companies being categorized as bad acquirers may disagree, a methodology exists that the academic community and the business media accept. Dozens, if not hundreds, of academic studies use the methodology I describe below and use throughout this book. The explanation may be somewhat heavy sledding, but it is, I think, worth the effort.

The fundamental model is called the Cumulative Abnormal Return model or Standard-Event Methodology and may be found in Hassan Tehranian and James Waegelein's article.

To establish whether an investment strategy is good, the researcher first computes the monthly common stock returns for each security in a sample. The researcher then statistically regresses these returns against the monthly returns of the market portfolio (Standard & Poor's 500) during the corresponding calendar months for each sample security. This is done in the months prior to announcement date of an acquisition, a new compensation plan, a new investment, or whatever. This "market model" procedure provides regression coefficients the researcher can use to estimate the expected security return in each month before and after the event.

The researcher then subtracts the expected return from the actual return in each month, and the resulting prediction error is a measure of the security's abnormal performance. In other words, one estimates the extent to which the stock price moved independently of the broad-based market. The theory assumes the abnormal return to have been the result of the acquisition or other event.

For example, assume the following:

How to Calculate Stock Price Movement Attributable to an Event

S&P 500 movement during the period:	7%
Estimated movement by Company XYZ during the same period*:	6%
Actual movement by Company XYZ during the period:	9%
Stock price movement attributable to the event:	3% (9% − 6%)

* Estimated using regression analysis on S&P 500 data and Company XYZ data prior to the event.

One can use these results to estimate a particular event's impact (an acquisition, for example) on shareholder value of the buying company. Assume the market value of Company XYZ was, say, $1 billion prior to acquiring another company, and its actual market value increase after the acquisition was $90 million (9 percent of $1 billion) to $1.09 billion. Of this amount, the general market movement would account for $60 million, and the acquisition would account for $30 million. Conversely, an event is considered to have a negative impact on shareholder value even if the company's stock price actually increased during the period. This would occur if the actual stock price increase was less than the predicted increase.

But why were corporate buyers motivated to undertake acquisitions that held so little true promise?

HOW EXECUTIVE STOCK OWNERSHIP AFFECTED TAKEOVERS

Aside from the traditional factors that motivated corporate buyers to undertake so many acquisitions in the last half of the 1980s, executive compensation plans—the emphasis on stock options rather than stock ownership—played an important role.

Michael Jensen and Kevin Murphy have argued in the *Harvard Business Review* that low executive stock ownership is a major problem in the strategies of major public corporations. They further found that as a percentage of total corporate value, CEO ownershp has never been very high. Looking at CEO stock ownership at the nation's 250 largest public companies, the CEO at the median point owns shares worth just over $2.4 million—less than 0.07 percent of the corporation's market value. Nine out of ten CEOs own less than 1 percent of their company stock, while fewer than one in twenty owns more than 5 percent.

John McConnel and Henri Servaes asked whether higher levels of executive ownership increased financial performance and raised shareholder value. They examined the relationship between the structure of the equity ownership—primarily insiders and institutional owners—and a financial measure called "Tobin's Q," looking at more than 1,000 companies in 1976 and 1,000 companies in 1986. Tobin's Q is the ratio of a company's market value to its book value. The higher the Q ratio, the more valuable the company is relative to its book assets. The McConnel and Servaes study showed that at almost every level, as insider ownership rises, the value of Q increases dramatically.

For an illustration of what this means, assume that Company ABC has a market value of $1 billion and a book value of $900 million; its Q ratio is 1.11 ($900 million divided by $1 billion). Assume that Company XYZ has a market value of $1 billion and a book value of $1.1 billion; its Q ratio is .991. The McConnel and Servaes study predicts that Company ABC would have insider ownership of, say, 30 percent and that Company XYZ would have significantly less insider ownership, say 10 percent. (I'm keeping the numbers simple to make the point clear.) Their study showed that increasing insider stock ownership tended to be associated with a rising Q ratio—market value exceeds book value because the market will pay a premium for the company. The company as a going business is worth more than its assets sold separately.

"Managers' natural tendency is to allocate the firm's resources in their own best interests, which may conflict with the interest of outside shareholders," wrote McConnel and Servaes. "As management's equity ownership increases, their interests are likely to coincide with shareholders'. The first of these forces has a negative effect on the value of the firm, whereas the second has a positive effect."

The 1976 figures found that at low levels of insider ownership, a 10 percent stock ownership increase was accompanied by a 10 percent increase in Q. By 1986, the relationship became dramatically stronger. At low levels of inside ownership, a 10 percent stock ownership increase yielded a 30 percent increase in Q. The McConnel and Servaes study emphasized the relationship at low ownership levels because above 50 percent ownership the company loses the takeover premium. When insiders (or family members) own more than half the company's stock they can block any takeover; without a takeover possible, there is no takeover premium. This study also found that relatively large institutional ownership is associated with relatively large executive ownership, perhaps because institutions like companies in which the executives own a lot of the stock.

The authors looked at the relationship between insider ownership and return on assets. Their statistical analysis showed that a higher level of return on assets is associated with higher levels of insider ownership. They also considered whether the causality works the other way; that is, do managers of successful firms tend to retain a large fraction of the corporation's stock? It may be that the successful corporations are more likely to reward their managers with more stock than the less successful firms. This is not supported by the fact that the Q ratio tends to flatten out at very high ownership levels. In other words, if successful firms tended to give their managers more stock, they would not stop at the 50 percent level, but would continue to give 60, 70, or 80 percent because the boards or the executives would continue to award themselves higher amounts as financial performance continued to improve. What actually happens, according to the data, is that above 50 percent ownership, a takeover premium no longer applies to the stock price, and there is nothing the executives can do to raise the stock price because the market will not reward their efforts. These data are consistent with the Hay Group studies of stock ownership presented in Chapter 2.

Do long-term incentive plans work to align the interests of management and shareholders, and are some plans better than others? This book argues that poor executive compensation plans, especially stock options, encouraged executives to undertake risky acquisitions. While I will demonstrate that this is indeed true, the first question is whether executive compensation plans "work," that is, do they motivate executives to grab the carrot that has been placed in front of them? In other words, do some compensation plans reduce the "agency problem"?

James A. Brickley, Sanjai Bhagat, and Ronald C. Lease, looking at eighty-three companies, found that the implementation of long-term incentive plans, including stock options, restricted stock, and long-term cash plans such as performance units, increased stock prices by 2.4 percent more than they would have without such plans. More significantly, stock option plans increased stock prices only 1.5 percent while other plans increased prices by more than 4 percent. This means that although shareholders believed the implementation of a stock option plan was better than nothing, they had real concerns about those plans relative to other schemes.

In a study more directly applicable to this book's thesis, Richard DeFusco and his associates studied what happened to a company's stock price after the firm implemented a stock option plan. They found that stock prices fell relative to the overall stock market for two-thirds of the firms in their sample. As DeFusco writes, "This suggests that an executive stock option plan motivates the manager to increase the variability of the firm's equity returns by investing in more risky projects." The table below shows the cumulative stock price declines for 359 companies for a number of years after the implementation of a stock option plan. This important finding indicates that the stock market expects executives under a stock option plan to undertake strategies that *reduce* the company's value.

Stock Price Change after Stock Option Plan Implementation

Years after Plan Implemented	STOCK PRICE CHANGE	
	Absolute	*Adjusted for Industry*
One	− 6.7%	− 3.2%
Two	−14.2	− 7.9
Three	−18.6	−10.1
Four	−25.9	−13.9
Five	−29.4	−14.7

Executives Must Be Driven in the Right Direction

Incentive plans do indeed change executive behavior. At a minimum, the shareholders *believe* these plans will change executive behavior with the expectation that they will ultimately improve operating results and increase market value. Because executives are driven by their compensation plans, these plans must be constructed to urge them toward appropriate shareholder goals—stock appreciation and dividends.

As I have been showing, stock options change executive behavior, but not in the desired direction. The model executive compensation plans at the end of this book (Chapter 7) will increase shareholder value more than the ordinary or traditional plans. While stock price movement around a new plan's announcement is based upon the market's expectation of improved (or diminished) performance, an executive compensation plan with a different philosophical foundation than most obsolete plans is more likely to help the stock's price than hurt it.

Stock options for executives have asymmetric risk profiles. Different risk profiles between two parties is always hazardous to the party having the "full risk" profile. The partner with the lower risk profile is generally motivated to attempt more risky ventures than the other party desires. By definition, a higher risk strategy has higher probability of failure; roll the dice often enough and high risk strategies will ultimately fail.

The savings and loan (S&L) crisis is a fascinating and important example of asymmetric risks. Robert Krulwich, a television reporter, traced "the trouble to the 1982 deregulation of savings and loans, which permitted them to invest their federally insured deposits in all manner of risky speculations," reported the *New York Times* in October, 1991. The S&Ls could underwrite highly speculative investments—primarily real estate and junk bonds—without fear of losing their investors' principal. If the junk bonds did well, the bank profited handsomely. If the bonds soured, losing interest and principal, the federal government stepped in to replace the principal. The federal government had all the downside risk (and, in contrast to shareholders and executives, none of the upside benefit), while the S&L owners had all the upside opportunity and little risk. This was a situation primed for disaster. As is the case for many human affairs, including executive compensation, individual risk profiles go a long way in explaining behavior.

When a corporation gives its executives their stock options for "free," the executives win if the stock price goes up and do not lose if the price goes down. If, however, the executives must give up some other form of cash compensation in exchange for the options, then the options are not "free," and this implies a downside risk. An executive might, for example, receive options rather than a cash bonus; to the extent that the options replace the cash, the executive has paid for the options. This is what International Multifoods did, as I show in Chapter 7. Cash compensation (salary plus bonus) at American corporations grew by a 9 percent annual compound rate during the 1980s, at the same time the prevalence and size of stock option and other executive compensation programs also grew dramatically. I believe, therefore, that corporations granted most options as "add-ons" that were, in fact, free; the executives did not give up any other compensation for them.

Figure 4-1 illustrates this issue. Efficient markets predict that a shareholder buys a security with essentially equal probability of profit and loss, that is, the complete "normal" distribution shown by the curve. An executive stock option holder experiences only the right, shaded, side of the figure, the profit-only side.

This one-sided risk profile, of course, does not hold for the regular shareholders or for the executives if they own large amounts of real stock in addition to or instead of their stock

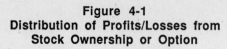

Figure 4-1
Distribution of Profits/Losses from
Stock Ownership or Option

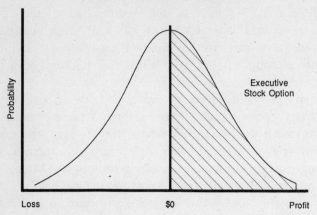

options. These shareholders actually lose money if the stock price goes down.

The buyers of publicly traded "call" options (for example, those traded on the Chicago Board of Options Exchange) also do not have one-sided risk profiles. Major newspapers publish the prices of outside options to purchase stock daily. The following, from the *New York Times,* defines an outside option:

Option Tables Explained

Options contracts to buy or sell 100 shares of a stock at a set price until a specified future date are traded in two forms. Call options give the holder the right to "call," or buy the stock. The price at which the option may be exercised is called the striking price. All options, both calls and puts, have a buyer and a "writer," or seller. The buyer of a call option anticipates a rise in the price of the underlying stock, while the writer usually does not expect the price of the underlying stock to reach the option's striking price.

As an example, the newspaper gave the following data on an *option* to buy one share of General Electric stock on October 20, 1991:

Company:	General Electric
Current Price of One Share:	$71.375
Strike Price:	$70.000
Expiration Date of Option:	March 1992
"Inherent" Value:	$ 1.375 ($71.375 − $70.000)
Price of Option:	$ 4.50
Net Value of Option:	$ 3.125

This shows the option's value. Since no equivalent market exists for executive options, we use a model to estimate the cash equivalent value of such option as described in the Appendix. The price these outside buyers pay for their options presumably does reflect downside risk. They can lose real value if the stock price does not rise sufficiently to cover their investment.

THE CONSEQUENCES OF DIFFERENT RISK PROFILES

Even under what might be considered ideal circumstances, executive shareholders should have different risk profiles from outside (nonemployee) shareholders. The executives have a much closer financial relationship to their companies than do outside shareholders. (Charlie Tharp from Bristol-Myers Squibb and my office-mate in graduate school pointed this out to me.) An outside shareholder can sever his or her relationship with the company with a phone call to a broker. In this sense, the shareholding executives are much less "liquid" than regular shareholders, since they cannot discontinue their relationship so instantaneously. For this reason alone, it is reasonable to believe they do not need to own massive amounts of stock to link their interests to the outside shareholders. Yet executives own very little stock, and because the executives own so few shares, they feel free to use the free cash flow in ways they might not if they were risking their own money. In particular, they have made inappropriate acquisitions that ultimately reduced shareholder value.

This means that the risk profiles of the two groups are very different—with different behavioral implications for the executives. The executives are motivated to undertake riskier strategies than the shareholders actually desire. One claim for stock options is that they motivate otherwise risk-averse executives to take prudent chances. Executives, in this argument, are risk averse because they have an undiversified portfolio; their financial and career opportunities are so closely linked to the fortunes of their companies that they do not want to take any chances at all.

I believe that options—as opposed to stock ownership—have swung the pendulum too far in the opposite direction. This risk-searching behavior manifests itself as a quest for investment opportunities that have very high potential payoffs (even if the payoff probability is relatively low). The clearest manifestation of this is one company taking over another.

Why did stock options drive inappropriate acquisitions in the last half of the 1980s and not earlier? In the early 1980s, the recovery of the economy in general and the stock market in particular, stemming from Reaganomics (tax cuts and government spending), was sufficient to increase the value of executive stock options dramatically. By the late 1980s the stock market engine was starting to lose steam, and both executives and institutional shareholders were driven to search for other ways to increase stock values.

Note that the institutional shareholders benefited handsomely from the purchase (acquisition) of the companies in which they held stock. The executives from the acquiring companies were motivated to make acquisitions to try to drive up their own stock prices. While an acquisition strategy generally failed as a way to increase the buying company's stock price, it was the only game in town, and there were of course some notable exceptions. Conagra bought Banquet Foods in 1980, and Conagra's shareholders saw the value of their stock rise by more than $300 million as the market perceived potential advantages between the two food companies to be quite large. Finally, there is good reason to believe that the conglomerate takeover craze of the 1960s—for example, LTV, ITT, and the like—may have been at least partly attributable to the stock options held by those executives.

The problem has been that there are few creative and effective alternatives to stock options, which has left boards of directors and their executive management teams with limited possibilities. Corporations have used stock options extensively if only because the Financial Accounting Standards Board has given options extremely favorable accounting treatment.* The goal of generating stock ownership among a group of employees, professional managers who had limited resources to purchase stock outright, was a difficult one.

Although I have saved the general solution to this dilemma for the last chapter, I must make a general macroeconomic point here: While stock options probably work during a broad-based worldwide economic upturn, they *compound* the problems associated with a broad-based economic stagnation. Generally speaking, it is, by definition, extremely difficult for executives to boost their stock's price in a stagnant economy and stock market. Stock options, as I am arguing, motivate executives to undertake excessively risky strategies, strategies that in a stagnant economy are less likely to pay off than if the economy were robust. When the strategies fail, it compounds the stagnation, as profits fall, financial losses mount, and more takeovers occur.

On the other hand, if the incentive plans encourage exec-

* This policy is currently under active review and may be changed shortly.

utives to undertake strategies appropriate for the economy, there will be a high probability they will pay off, the companies will be profitable, they will not lay off employees, and they will help shorten the trough in the business cycle.

WHY COMPANIES WILL PAY LOWER PRICES FOR ACQUISITIONS

The search for continuing stock price improvement was so difficult during the latter half of the 1980s that shareholder and executive interests should have been much more closely aligned than they were during the first half when the rising stock market tended to mask the problems. An upswing in the business cycle and general rise in the stock market increases the probability that an acquisitions strategy—any acquisitions strategy—will pay off. Further, there is reason to believe (and my consulting experience supports this point) that executives resist transferring risk from the shareholders to themselves.

Nevertheless, corporations, their shareholders, and their executives will gain major economic benefits from the type of alignment I recommend. Linking shareholder and executive risk profiles should result in more appropriate executive investment behavior, including acquisitions and balancing short- and long-term interests. It will also address the agency problem, balancing management and shareholder concerns. Specifically, if an organization takes this balanced risk approach, one outcome will be more appropriate acquisitions; the company will pay lower prices than it would have paid or not make the purchase at all. Given the other potential benefits from takeovers—improved operating efficiencies, synergistic strategies, and all the rest—lower acquisition prices will generate major economic advantages.

Obviously, while the target company shareholders will suffer somewhat because the acquiring company pays a lower price than it might have paid, the buying company shareholders gain more than proportionately because their company has not paid too much. This is the fundamental definition of improved economic efficiency, which economists call "Pareto Optimality." The benefits to one party or to society as a whole are greater than the aggregate losses of the other party. If properly structured, the buying company's executives could be major beneficiaries as well, in the form of increased wealth, reduced risk, and heightened job security.

Note that stock options are not alone in their pernicious effects. Other forms of executive compensation plans—particularly long-term cash plans, frequently called performance unit plans—may similarly have turned executives toward negative return investments. There are two possible reasons why this should be. First, these plans are generally based on accounting profits, three-year cumulative profits, for example, or three-year average return on equity. Studies of corporate finance—Bennet Stewart's *The Quest for Value* is one—have demonstrated how it is possible to increase reported earnings while simultaneously reducing shareholder value, since the returns are below the cost of capital. Second, studies have shown that executive pay can be closely linked to the size of the company, irrespective of the company's profitability. Again investments can increase the company's size—even increase profits—without increasing true economic or shareholder value.

Naturally, there are some checks and balances on this risk-seeking behavior. The board of directors does examine management's strategies. But, given management's superior knowledge plus the general uncertainties of managing large and complex organizations, monitoring is extraordinarily difficult and boards can be misled about or are unfamiliar with problems. Also, the executive's desire for job security checks the most outrageous adventures. If a chief executive officer's strategy continuously or chronically fails, the executive's job becomes, as they say, at risk.

EXECUTIVE STOCK OPTIONS/OWNERSHIP AND ACQUISITIONS

I have begged the question: How and why do executive stock options and the lack of actual stock ownership drive bad acquisitions? Further, can I demonstrate a relationship between options and the success or failure of an acquisition strategy?

"Executive stock options may also cause managers to take on more risk. The asymmetric payoffs of call options make it more attractive for managers to undertake risky projects," wrote Richard DeFusco in a 1990 study. This study demonstrates that the adoption of stock option plans increases the stock price variance of the companies that offer them by 16 percent. The stock market, in other words, believes that after a company implements such a plan the stock price, reflecting an increase in managerial risk-taking, will become very volatile.

Graef Crystal, writing in *Fortune* magazine in 1990, found direct statistical proof that increasing the volatility of a company's stock yielded a higher level of expected compensation. If beta increases from 1 to 1.1, then CEO pay tends to rise by 4 percent. Beta measures a stock's relative volatility compared to the overall market. For example, if the market increases or declines by 10 percent, the stock of a company with a beta of 1.00 would also increase or decline by 10 percent. If the company's beta is 2.00, its stock price would increase or decline by 20 percent in such a market; if the beta is 0.50, the price would increase or decline by 5 percent. Crystal's study supports our contention that stock options motivate executives to increase their stock's volatility by searching for riskier strategies.

A 1985 study by Wilber Lewelleen and his associates examined "whether the impact of a merger on bidder firm stock returns is more likely to be negative when management's ownership of the firm's stock is small. . . . We conjecture that managers whose equity ownership positions in their firms are large are likely to be especially careful about the share price impact of the mergers they arrange; they should less frequently put their firms through shareholder-wealth-decreasing acquisitions than managers whose equity stakes in their companies are small." This study divided 191 acquisitions into two groups: those creating positive returns to the buying company's shareholders—the "good" acquirers—and those with negative returns. It found that the management of the good acquirers owned two to four times as much stock as the poor acquirers. This held whether the measure was the percentage of total shares management owned or a ratio of the value of the stock owned to cash compensation (another valid way to measure executive stock ownership).

This is a profound story. Lack of stock ownership and large amounts of stock options appear to motivate managers to make poor acquisitions. These managers tend to make acquisitions for reasons that at best have little to do with shareholder interests and at worst reduce shareholder value.

CAUSES AND COSTS OF DIVERSIFICATION

Amar Bhide's 1990 study, "Reversing Corporate Diversification," brought together the issues of diversification, financial takeover specialists, and executive stock options/ ownership, discussing the advantages and disadvantages of large diversified corporations. While the study's main substance is outside this book's scope, it does raise several salient points.

One basic problem with a large diversified company is that it is difficult, if not impossible, to provide large amounts of equity ownership to the chief executive officer. Bhide makes the critical assumption that if chief executive officers own large amounts of stock they will behave differently than if they do not own much stock. They will operate effectively to make their companies more profitable. Since large diversified companies cannot give significant equity ownership to their senior executives, they provide them with stock options instead. Stock options are an "imperfect substitute for significant equity ownership," Bhide writes.

First, stock options create an incentive for managers to maximize stock price rather than total returns. For example, because dividend payments cause share prices to be lower than they would otherwise be, managers may choose to retain cash in the firm rather than paying it out as dividends—even when attractive investment opportunities are not available.

Second, options give managers an incentive to make risky investments. Consider, for example, the CEO of a railroad who expects to retire in five years and whose stock is not expected to do much of anything during that period. Suppose it is early 1986, oil prices have fallen to $15 a barrel and an investment banker recommends the acquisition of an oil company that will look terrific if oil prices rise above $30 a barrel (but not otherwise). While shareholders might balk, the CEO's stock options will give him a strong incentive to go through with the acquisition. If oil prices do rise, so will the value of his options; if they don't, the CEO has little to lose; at worst, his options will expire unexercised. In other words, incentives may get misaligned because, although shareholders can gain or lose real money, managers who own options enjoy only the upside of changes in the price of their stock.

The third and major point Bhide makes is that unraveling diversified companies probably makes economic sense.

External capital markets have come of age, while there has been no evidence of a corresponding improvement in the functioning of internal corporate hierarchies. The diversified firm is, therefore, a less valuable institution than it might once have been. And as a practical matter, because investors today are more concentrated and enjoy broader investment opportunities, they are less tolerant of an organizational form that reflects managerial desires to perpetuate growth (often for growth's sake) and achieve financial self-sufficiency.

ARE STOCK OPTIONS SUCCESSFUL IN OTHER REGARDS?

Stock options encourage risk, diversification, and growth, often without creating shareholder value. It is a major conclusion that the diversified company, too, probably needs alternatives to stock options to manage, and corporations need incentives that will encourage the creation of shareholder value rather than pure growth. The other implication is that the conglomerate is really not a viable economic form, and to operate the diversified company in today's environment probably requires strong quasi-independent divisions and strong incentives at the division level.

Are options successful in other regards? "They are more popular and lucrative than ever, but they don't do what they are supposed to do, and the cost might shock shareholders if they knew it," wrote Thomas A. Stewart in *Fortune* magazine at the beginning of 1990.

> Options don't really make managers walk in the owners' moccasins. Only after executives exercise options do they truly become owners. Until then they have no capital at risk, and if the stock sags, they can expect a new grant the next year at a lower price. Some companies even cancel "underwater" options and replace them with new ones. Many did so after the October 1987 market crash.

Stewart's article quoted a study by James H. Carbone, a management consultant in Novato, California. The study found that "companies without option plans did as well as companies with them." Carbone looked at 180 companies and ten measures of corporate performance and found no statistical relationship between performance and stock option compensation.

Further evidence of a gap between those who hold options and regular shareholders comes from compensation expert Graef S. Crystal, who studied the option gains of 130 CEOs from 1986 to 1988. Crystal tracked the CEO's option profits against the company's stock appreciation, reasoning that the two ought to move together. Instead, his regression analysis yielded an extremely weak correlation: Only about one-seventh of the CEO's profit could be explained by the stock's movement. Most came from bigger grants or from other factors, such as the time when the CEO exercised the option or the corporation's replacing underwater options. In short, the CEO's option compensation is far out of proportion with what ordinary shareholders get from rising stock prices.

"Option holders must become regular shareholders eventually, when they exercise their options, but most apparently get right off that bus by selling the shares and pocketing the spread in cash," Crystal wrote in *Fortune* in 1990. "But executives who cash out all their shares are saying that they consider other investments better than one in their own company."

My own statistical analysis of executive stock options and executive stock ownership found they play a role in influencing executive behavior in acquisitions. In 1988, economists at the Securities and Exchange Commission conducted a famous study entitled "Do Bad Bidders Make Good Targets?" This study examined a large number of acquisitions and again divided them into successful acquiring firms and unsuccessful acquiring firms. The former were much more likely to themselves ultimately become the target of an acquisition because they were weakened by their purchases. For my purposes, the study is valuable because the SEC examined the companies and their deals in detail. I selected the ten most successful and the ten least successful acquirers. These two groups allowed me to examine one critical issue directly: Namely, are the executives with large stock options or low stock ownership trying to increase—consciously or unconsciously—their stock price's *volatility* by buying firms with greater stock price volatility than their own company's stock? If the answer is yes, I have some proof that options do foster managerial behavior that is not in the shareholders' interests.

The measure I use for stock price volatility is beta. Utility company betas are less than 1.00, and bio-technology company betas are well above 1.00. The table below summarizes what I found.

Successful acquirers, in other words, saw their stock price rise on average 8.3 percent more than the general market movement while unsuccessful acquirers saw their stock fall 5.4 percent.

While these statistical data are indicative rather than definitive, one can draw some interesting and important inferences. First, there appears to be a dramatic difference between good and bad acquirers. There is a difference of almost 14 percentage points in their market values after the

How Successful Acquirers Compare to Unsuccessful Acquirers

	Successful Acquirers	*Unsuccessful Acquirers*
Percent change in stock price*	8.3%	(5.4%)
Ratio of betas (target/acquired)	83%	108%
Percent of total shares owned (CEO)	1.4%	0.7%
Ratio of share value to TCC (CEO)†	6.1 : 1	4.3 : 1
Ratio of options to shares owned (CEO)	1.6 : 1	8.3 : 1

* Excess stock price movement (above or below general market movement) from five days before to one day after the acquisition's announcement.

† TCC = total cash compensation (base salary plus annual bonus).

acquisitions occurred. This means that if the buyer's market value was $1 billion before the acquisition, a bad acquirer ended at $950 million and a good acquirer ended at $1.08 billion. It is also essential to remember that the bad acquirers were themselves much more likely to become takeover targets.

The CEOs of the good acquirers owned dramatically more stock—as a share of total shares outstanding, they owned more than twice as much as the CEOs of the poor acquirers. Also, the "good" CEOs owned 50 percent more shares as a multiple of total cash compensation—indicating higher relative cash compensation for the good CEOs. This higher cash compensation may indicate higher levels of financial performance, the primary driver of cash compensation. Again, as we will see in the last chapter, the ratio of the value of the CEO's stock to total cash compensation is an excellent measure of how closely linked the CEO is to the shareholders. As I've noted, at most large companies, with their enormous market values, the CEOs, even the richest ones, cannot afford a large percentage of the total shares. Second, if the ratio is 10:1, a 10 percent increase in stock price will double an executive's total potential and realized compensation and a 10 percent decline will wipe it out.

The most dramatic results are the option and beta analysis. The CEOs of the bad acquirers have significantly higher ratios of options to stock, 8.3 to 1 versus 1.6 to 1 for the good acquirers. This indicates they have the potential to benefit dramatically from a rising stock price without any downside risk. In their hunt for higher volatility for their company's stock price, they may seek acquisitions that will increase that volatility.

The relative betas support this hypothesis. While the sample size is limited, and the relative size of two companies could be important, the data suggest that the good acquirers make beta-reducing acquisitions and the bad acquirers make beta-increasing acquisitions.

WHAT ELSE MOTIVATES AN ACQUISITION STRATEGY?

The business press has argued that executives pursue an acquisition strategy because it is a win-win situation. If the acquisition (or any strategy for that matter) succeeds, the executives get rich. If the strategy fails and their own companies are taken over, the executives are protected by their golden parachutes or other forms of security the board of directors provides. While the press usually makes this argument with respect to targets, it can apply to corporate buyers as well. This argument is one of the few the business press makes that has some validity. It makes the risk profile argument that much more skewed against the shareholders. The shareholders need protection from management's golden parachutes.

In addition to increasing the potential value of their options, are there other purely managerial motivations for acquisitions? Several academic studies have asked this question. Randall Morck and his associates gave some important answers in "Characteristics of Targets of Hostile and Friendly Takeovers." Obviously, if the executives themselves are large shareholders, a buying company's shareholders can be assured (there are no guarantees) that the firm will pursue only value-increasing acquisitions. Even if these owner-executives have other reasons to pursue acquisitions, at least one reason—even if not the primary reason—will be to increase shareholder value. If the executives are not large shareholders, the external, or public, shareholders do have reason for concern. To the extent that managers pursue acquisitions for reasons other than to increase shareholder value, they may be motivated to pay more for a target company than pure economic reasons can justify. And this, in the final analysis, is what causes acquisitions to fail. The success of a synergistic strategy or cost cutting or new distribution or whatever depends considerably on the target company's purchase price. At some point, the target company costs too much, and the cost reductions or distribution efficiencies required to make the acquisition profitable are unattainable.

Bruce Wasserstein, the former co-head of mergers and acquisitions at First Boston Corporation and current CEO of Wasserstein-Perella (an investment banking boutique known for its takeover advice), believed that if his clients wanted to be global players in an industry, they had to "pay the price." This meant in practice that it was all right to overpay for an acquisition, *Forbes* magazine reported, because in a rising stock market a company could always locate a buyer who would pay more for the acquisition. But the stock market basically stopped rising in October 1987, and the junk bond market collapsed in 1989. If managerial objectives do drive acquisitions, especially in situations in which the managers own little stock, overpayment becomes tragic for the buying company's shareholders.

But what are these managerial objectives in addition to or instead of maximization of shareholder value? They include growth, diversification, and a history of poor performance, according to Randall Morck.

Growth. A number of academic and business press articles have argued that managers pursue growth strategies even if they do not increase economic value. Morck's data showed that corporations that bought slower-growing targets made much better acquisitions than those that bought fast-growing targets. This suggests that poor acquirers were trying to "buy" growth. Why? Growth increases the likelihood of the company's survival in its current corporate form since size alone deters takeover. Growth also increases the promotional opportunities of junior executives and can be part of a strategy to recruit and retain superior executive talent. Finally, growth can be part of a strategy to increase compensation.

Diversification. Managers are motivated to pursue diversification even if it hurts shareholder value. It allows them to diversify their own financial portfolios to the extent they have stock or options. In addition, the more diversified a company, the harder it is for the board of directors to monitor executive performance. Executives of diversified corporations have more specific firm knowledge and are therefore more critical to the board. The empirical data support Morck's hypothesis. Shareholders of a buying company do much better when their managers buy companies related to the firm's core business than when they buy unrelated businesses.

It is interesting to observe that financial takeover specialists almost always acquire companies in unrelated industries. The clear difference here is that financial buyers are generally sole proprietors or closely held partnerships or corporations, so they are unwilling to overpay for their targets.

Historically poor performance by the buyer. It is conceivable corporations make bad acquisitions because the managers simply make bad decisions. If they perform poorly historically, they may try to make acquisitions in industries in which they hope they can improve their financial performance. They may be making value-destroying acquisitions even if they are buying higher levels of *accounting* profits, since the profits could be below their capital cost. Once again, Morck's data show that good buyers have significantly higher levels of financial performance relative to their targets than do poor buyers.

"To the extent that acquisitions serve these objectives, managers of bidding firms are willing to pay more for targets than they are worth to bidding firms' shareholders," Morck has written. In any acquisition, the initial price paid predicts ultimate success. Reading the business press, one is struck by the number of times that financial takeover specialists remark that they had to back away from an acquisition because they believed that the ultimate price paid by the acquiring company was too high.

"Option-motivated" or other forms of risk-seeking behavior do not, of course, always result in reduced shareholder value. As I demonstrated by the General Electric example, corporate buyers *do* make successful acquisitions outside their core businesses. In addition, even within my statistical data, there were companies in which executives with large stock options made successful acquisitions. If the acquisition strategies of companies where the executives had options *always* failed, boards of directors or the executives themselves would eventually learn that lesson from the market.

For whatever reasons, ranging from an appropriate (that is, low) price or truly large potential synergies, the stock market may perceive a company has made a real value-adding acquisition and drive up the stock price. Du Pont and Bristol-Myers, which use stock options significantly, are generally recognized as extremely successful companies that have made major acquisitions (Conoco and Squibb, respectively). Nevertheless, are there material differences between the compensation programs of good acquirers and poor acquirers?

While I could find no academic study that asked this exact question, I found another study that pursued a related issue. Mitchell Langbert examined the differences in the compensation programs at a group of excellent companies and a group of "least admired" companies. Financial and stock price performance were among the attributes that determined whether a company was designated as excellent or least admired. Langbert found that executive compensation at the excellent companies had two key characteristics:

1. These executives received much more compensation from profits from stock option exercise than the executives at the least admired companies.
2. Compensation at the excellent companies was much more closely linked to the riskiness of their stock prices (beta again) than was compensation at the least admired companies.

These two findings show that executives at excellent companies have their option profits positively (and statistically significantly) related to beta, that is, the riskiness of their stock. It is also important to note that least admired companies have their option profits negatively (and statistically significantly) related to increases in their beta, or riskiness. Figure 4-2 illustrates this. It shows that as the risk (that is, beta) increases for a company, option profits increase at excellent companies and decrease at least admired companies. Since a company's stock price must increase for the executives to make a profit on their options, the shareholders of these excellent companies are "winning" as well. While Langbert's study did not focus on acquisitions, the general search for risk in all competitive strategies does yield a payoff

Figure 4-2
Relationship Between Option Profits and Beta

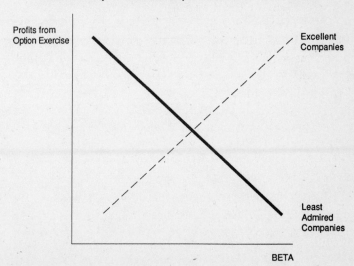

Source: Langbert, Mitchell "In Search of Compensation: A Compensation of Executives in Peters and Waterman's Excellent and Fortune's Least Admired Firms," *Benefits Quarterly*, Second Quarter 1990.

for executives at certain excellent companies, and their share-holders benefit proportionately. This search is counterproductive at companies that are otherwise considered least admired. Since there are far fewer excellent companies than others, this risk-seeking approach to compensation, where the shareholders bear most of the risk, is generally not advisable.

This has been an important story. In the search for causes and consequences of the 1980s takeover craze, the entire media, plus most business analysts and academics, missed the role of executive pay completely. The crisis is not with the *levels* of executive pay, but with stock options that moved executives from being risk averse to seeking *more* risk than the shareholders desired. Stock options are, for most companies, a less than ideal solution. But before describing the solution to this crisis, we need to make two detours—to the world of institutional investors and to that of accountants and lawyers.

CHAPTER 5

JUNK BONDS, INSTITUTIONAL SHAREHOLDER ACTIVISM, AND EXECUTIVE COMPENSATION

> *The nation's largest public-employee pension fund is taking aim at salaries paid top executives of companies with weak earnings records.*
> —*Wall Street Journal,* December 10, 1990

INSTITUTIONAL SHAREHOLDERS, especially pension funds, both gained and lost from the takeover craze, depending upon whether they owned the stock of the target company or the buying company. As I showed in the last chapter, executive compensation plays a key role in predicting the outcome of takeovers—that is, whether they are beneficial or harmful to shareholders. For the 1990s, institutional shareholders will take a more active role in executive pay issues to try to repeat their stock market gains of the 1980s.*

NOTE: This chapter covers the current state of corporate governance, shareholder activism, and their impact on executive pay. As this book goes to press rapid change is occurring with respect to SEC disclosure requirements, the treatment of shareholder proposals, and valuing accounting for stock options. Although some of my comments may already be out-of-date, the key dynamics behind corporate governance relationships remain unchanged.
* I want to thank Robert C. Ochsner for his invaluable contribution to this chapter. Diane Lerner provided critical research.

141

The *Wall Street Journal* quote heralds a revolution in management-shareholder relations. What was historically a cozy or supportive relationship, depending on your perspective, has become a negotiating relationship at best, or an antagonistic one at worst. This chapter covers four issues regarding the new shareholder "activism."

1. What has changed from the 1980s to the 1990s? Junk bonds served to discipline management during the 1980s. Financial takeover specialists used high-yield securities (junk bonds) to buy large companies. Institutional shareholders benefited significantly from those takeovers. Mergers tended to provide superior returns either from firms being taken over or from firms acting to avoid being taken over.

2. With the junk bond market's collapse, institutional shareholders will try to use corporate governance generally, and executive pay specifically, to try to raise stock market returns. The financial takeover specialists have disappeared.

3. The proxy-voting process and the disclosure process will serve as the mechanisms for shareholders to put pressure on management.

4. I make specific recommendations about disclosure issues that attempt to balance the needs of all sides. In the final analysis, however, executive pay plans must be structured to motivate managers to create economic value.

CORPORATE GOVERNANCE NEEDS AN OVERHAUL

As we move through the 1990s, we could be witnessing a major change in corporate governance, a change spurred by shareholder discontent with the current process.

In theory, the corporate governance process exists to protect shareholder interests. After all, the structure provides for a board of directors, elected by and accountable to the shareholders, that is supposed to monitor management activities. On paper, this structure provides for a flow of information between the shareholders, the board of directors, and the management team. This communication should result in decisions that support the corporation's and its shareholders' long-term best interests.

In fact, corporate governance does not work that way. Institutional shareholders believe we have experienced a serious breakdown in the process that can be broadly attributed to an imbalance in the key interrelationships. There is too much distance between the board of directors and the shareholders, and too little between the board and management. This imbalance may have rendered the current process ineffective. Whether this is perception or reality, it needs to be addressed.

The big question is whether the process simply needs to be made more effective or whether it needs to be fundamentally changed. To answer this question and to develop appropriate solutions, we first must understand why the corporate governance relationships are out of balance and what factors are driving change. To do this, I will explore the dynamics behind what I consider the five key players in corporate governance: the boards of directors, management teams, shareholders, and the two big outside influences—the capital markets and the Securities and Exchange Commission.

Executive compensation, which has been called the "smoking gun" of poor corporate governance, will probably be the focus of the anticipated shareholder challenge. Why? Because, while other issues may be more important, shareholders can easily relate to how much executives earn. And press coverage of CEO pay excesses keeps the topic at the front of the shareholders' minds. Many CEO pay critics cite the implications of excessive compensation in light of our increasingly global economy; they express concerns about our global competitiveness given that American CEOs earn substantially more on average than do their European and Japanese counterparts.

Given that such critics are likely to use executive compensation as the catalyst for corporate governance change, I have focused my comments on the problems with today's corporate governance process on executive pay issues specifically.

The Board of Directors. Primary responsibility for corporate governance has long resided with the board of directors, whose role is to review management's strategic and operating business decisions and to represent the interests of the shareholders.

At one time, serving on a corporate board as an outside director was considered an honor, with compensation to match. The perception was that directors listened to various reports, rubber-stamped resolutions, ate lunch, and left. Supporting this perception has been the fact that many U.S. board members are not truly "outsiders" or independent of the company. Very often, the chairman of the board also happens to be the chief executive officer—clearly not an outsider. Also questionable as outsiders are the company's banker, lawyer, suppliers, and key customers. These, as the Working Group on Corporate Governance pointed out in the *Harvard Business Review,* board members often have a significant economic relationship with the company.

Another source of outside directors are the CEOs of other firms. Norman Macrae reported in *Business Month* that CEOs comprise over three-fifths of the outside directors of the top 1,000 U.S. companies. While CEOs may be considered truly outsiders, they certainly do not have a great deal of spare time. Further, they may have a vested interest in seeing high pay for other corporate CEOs because it gives them ammunition when they negotiate with their own boards. Macrae summed up the overall state of affairs with the following observation, "Most U.S. boards have become nothing more than mutual protection societies of chief executive officers."

Regardless of the degree of truth in this perception, a proliferation of shareholder lawsuits has caused a change in director activities. The lawsuits underscored the significant responsibilities directors carry. As a result, directors have become more active in their role of protecting shareholder interests. Shareholder activism has outpaced director activism, however, as large institutional shareholders have begun to step forward to say, "It's not enough. More direct shareholder involvement is needed; let's start with executive compensation."

The board's defense is that a process for setting executive compensation through the compensation committee exists, and "the system isn't broke, so there's no need to fix it." And model compensation committees do exist that force senior managers to earn their pay by rewarding shareholders, but they seem to be scarce. While controversial in its pay level, Disney is an example of such a model.

The counterargument is that compensation committees on the whole have not been very effective. CEOs quite appropriately take a strong leadership in compensation matters. Too often, the compensation committee is nothing more than a compliant extension of the CEO. This "rubber stamp" image is probably as strong for compensation committees as for any aspect of board operations.

Several conditions exist that make it very difficult for board compensation committees to address executive compensation proposals aggressively. First, the fact that many board members are not outsiders or are CEOs themselves makes it awkward for them to tackle CEO pay issues. Second, the complexity of today's executive compensation packages makes scrutiny difficult unless one happens to be a specialist in the field—which most board members are not. Typically, the CEO directs that consultants be engaged and prepare competitive studies, analyses of various incentive vehicles, and valuation methodologies. The complexity of the issues, conflicting interests, lack of expert advice, and time and staff constraints have all made it difficult for board

compensation committees to deal with executive pay satis-
factorily.

Further, while boards have to deal with intense and active
participation by company management when they address
executive pay, they have heard virtually nothing from the
shareholders. This imbalance has made the board's role in
representing shareholder interests even more precarious.
Why have the shareholders been silent?

The Shareholders. The most dramatic changes in corporate
governance are occurring because there has been a profound
shift in the shareholders' role. This shift is based on two
factors: increased institutional ownership, and a change in
the capital markets. These have combined to end generations
of shareholder silence on corporate governance and executive pay.

Who is today's typical shareholder? Equity ownership is
no longer spread among a legion of small investors. Block
ownership by institutional investors is the rule, not the exception. As of 1988, institutional investors held 47 percent of
the equity in the top 1,000 corporations, and an estimated 45
percent of all equities. As the table on page 147 shows, just
ten pension funds hold 6 percent of all U.S. equities.

Some industries tend to have higher concentrations of institutional ownership. Carolyn Kay Brancato found that the
aerospace, paper, and transportation industries lead the way
with 58 percent institutional ownership, while utilities and
telecommunications were the lowest at 35 percent. Because
of their increasing assets and concentrated power, institutions
are now looking to do something with that ownership. The
simplest strategy, namely to sell the stock of an underperforming company, is generally *not* available to large institutional shareholders. As *Fortune* says ". . . the sheer size of the
holding could make it difficult to unload without driving
down the price."

Institutions are responding to pressure from their owners

The Big Ten of the Pension World

Fund	Assets (in billions)	Percent in Equities	Share of U.S. Equity Market
TIAA-CREF (national teachers retirement system)	$ 95	35.7%	1.1%
California Public Employees Retirement System	58	36.0	0.6
New York State & Local Retirement Systems	45	47.0	0.7
American Telephone & Telegraph	42	51.0	0.7
General Motors*	41	43.8	0.6
New York City Retirement Systems	39	48.0	0.6
California State Teachers Retirement System	32	41.0	0.4
General Electric	31	42.0	0.4
New Jersey Division of Investment	27	50.0	0.5
International Business Machines†	27	43.8	0.4
TOTAL	$437	43.8%†	6.0%

* *Fortune* magazine estimates.
† Average.

to match the superior performance of the 1980s. They are looking beyond corporate finance to company operations, putting additional pressure on management. However, the reality is that the market is unlikely to triple again in the 1990s. Lower inflation, lower interest rates, the collapse of the junk bond market, and a slower economy will make it more difficult to achieve double-digit returns at low risk.

At one time, institutional investing was dominated by large banks, and investing was more personalized. Now it is considerably more global and impersonal. Global investing eliminates much of the personal aspect by a lack of proximity. The type of pressure that a remote investor can put on an underperforming company tends to more intense than, say, what the local bank can exert on a local company with familiar management. Unless a major political upheaval takes place, this global trend will be irreversible for ten to twenty years.

Institutional owners have significant clout that they now want to exert on the issue of executive pay. But, it is important to note, institutional ownership is not a brand-new phenomenon of the 1990s. These same institutional owners were indifferent to internal corporate governance issues throughout the 1980s. Instead of involving themselves, they were able to rely on "efficient markets" concepts that sanctioned a basically reactive posture. That is, these institutions received good returns without involving themselves with corporate governance. What has changed?

The Capital Markets. While some executive pay plans may have even discouraged top management from maximizing value for shareholders, fortunately for the individual and institutional investors, the capital markets had a vehicle that allowed value to be released anyway. The high-yield or "junk" bond provided a mechanism to do this in two ways. First, and most obviously, it was used by financial takeover specialists such as Ronald Perelman (CEO of Pantry Pride at the time) to take over much larger companies (Revlon) at a significant premium for the shareholders. There are countless other examples of this, including R. J. Reynolds and Singer. Second, and perhaps more importantly, these high-yield bonds created the constant threat to incumbent managements; they could be taken over by virtually anyone, not just a domestic or foreign rival or a major conglomerate. This served to discipline management. They tried to deliver as much value to shareholders as possible including stock repurchases, special dividends, tax-free spinoffs of noncore subsidiaries, management buyouts at a premium, and more. All this restructuring was in place of value-reducing or cash-absorbing strategies, especially poorly designed acquisitions. (For the full story of the value of junk bonds, see Glen Yago, *Junk Bonds*.)

By 1990, however, the junk bond market was dead. The collapse of Drexel Burnham Lambert and the incarceration of Michael Milken may or may not have been well deserved as retribution for the moral and economic excesses of the 1980s. Nevertheless, the external discipline that they provided for shareholders died along with their collapse. Shareholders, especially institutional shareholders, lost the primary vehicle in the bond market that released the value in the equity/stock markets. The stock market's 300 percent increase between 1980 and 1990 will not be easily repeated. What alternatives are available to shareholders? The most obvious is direct intervention in the corporate governance process, including a more direct linkage of executive pay-for-performance, especially the creation of economic value or shareholder value, including increasing free cash flow.

The Securities and Exchange Commission. While the capital market was, in my view, the principal reason for shareholder silence on executive pay, it was not the only factor. The SEC's position on disclosure and oversight has also changed. The primary form of shareholder disclosure has been proxy statements. But, as Nell Minnow, the president of Institutional Shareholder Services, Inc., observed before the Senate Oversight Committee in May 1991, "the proxies do not fully disclose CEO pay, or else require plodding through 19 pages of mind-numbing text to find all the different places that the portions of his compensation are listed."

Moreover, the SEC has historically disallowed shareholder

challenges to boards of directors over executive pay because it has deemed the size and nature of executive compensation to constitute ordinary business and therefore within the board's province. Thus, shareholders have not had much success in challenging executive pay issues. As Nell Minnow stated, "Their information is limited and difficult to use, and their oversight is even more limited and difficult to use." No wonder they relied upon the capital markets while they could.

Recently, we have seen the SEC's stance shift. The commission now considers three subjects involving remuneration to transcend ordinary business because "they raise important policy concerns" and are thus permissible topics for shareholders to discuss. These areas include golden parachutes, more detailed information on executive pay, and the ability to create a shareholder advisory committee that can advise the board on executive pay. These provisions are subject to various state law approvals, which may still disallow action on any one or all three.

Even these recent changes in the SEC's position do not affect the poor quality of basic executive pay information that corporations make available through the proxy disclosure process. I will focus on this specific area in my comments on corporate governance reform.

SURVEY OF CHAIRMEN OF COMPENSATION COMMITTEES

How do key board members feel about the success of executive pay plans in the corporate governance process? In 1990, The Hay Group conducted a survey of seventy executives who serve as the chairman of the compensation committee of a board of directors, or its equivalent, at some of the most prestigious companies in the United States. Our objective was to solicit the opinions of these business leaders regarding the purposes, effectiveness, and perceived value of the executive compensation programs they oversee on behalf of corporate shareholders.

The results illustrate the broad, thoughtful perspective one would expect from individuals who are closely involved with the most direct application of executive compensation. The responses of these board members reveal their deep concern that financial and organizational results may not fully match expectations, confirming the feelings of many professionals that existing executive compensation plans are more effective in producing short-term rather than long-term results.

Interestingly, these chairmen also share the view that "shareholder interests" go far beyond raising the stock price or creating shareholder value. They cite, for example, the practical importance of attracting and retaining superior talent and inspiring successful teamwork as important considerations in executive compensation plans.

They universally agreed that compensation plans should link employee and shareholder interests, especially for executives; most felt that the plans they monitor are doing a "good job" in this regard. In their view, shareholder interests are more broadly defined than might be expected. From the company perspective, these chairmen feel executive compensation programs are most helpful in providing these basic items. They also feel that the compensation programs they monitor are very effective in bettering the corporate financial performance they are designed to improve—with the most commonly used measures being earnings per share and return on equity.

Regarding the effectiveness of various traditional vehicles in linking employee and shareholder interests, the participants gave the responses shown in Figure 5-2. The significantly low ratings of stock appreciation rights (only 26 percent strongly agreed they do a good job of linking compensation with shareholder interest) and restricted stock (only 15 percent) clearly indicate a strong stewardship of shareholder interests by these chairmen; they obviously recognize these vehicles' shortcomings.

In these executives' opinions, the primary source of exec-

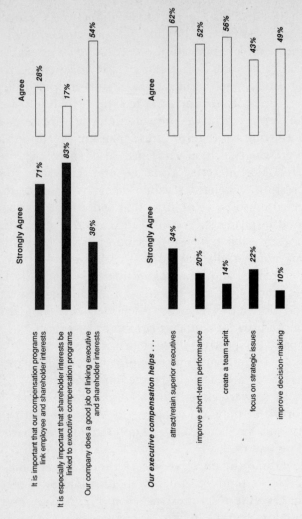

Figure 5-1
Compensation Committee Chairmen Views

Strongly Agree | **Agree**

It is important that our compensation programs link employee and shareholder interests — 71% / 28%

It is especially important that shareholder interests be linked to executive compensation programs — 83% / 17%

Our company does a good job of linking executive and shareholder interests — 38% / 54%

Our executive compensation helps . . .

Strongly Agree | **Agree**

attract/retain superior executives — 34% / 62%

improve short-term performance — 20% / 52%

create a team spirit — 14% / 56%

focus on strategic issues — 22% / 43%

improve decision-making — 10% / 49%

Source:1990 The Hay Group "Survey of Compensation Committee Chairmen."

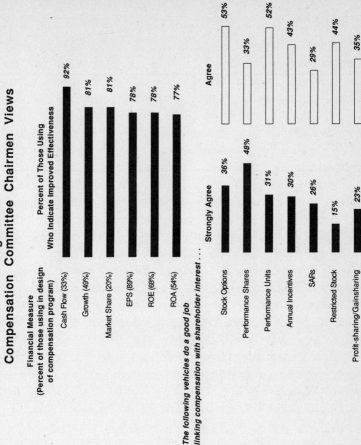

Figure 5-2
Compensation Committee Chairmen Views

Financial Measure
(Percent of those using in design of compensation program)

Percent of Those Using Who Indicate Improved Effectiveness

- Cash Flow (33%) — 92%
- Growth (49%) — 81%
- Market Share (20%) — 81%
- EPS (89%) — 78%
- ROE (68%) — 78%
- ROA (54%) — 77%

The following vehicles do a good job linking compensation with shareholder interest . . . .

Strongly Agree

- Stock Options — 36%
- Performance Shares — 48%
- Performance Units — 31%
- Annual Incentives — 30%
- SARs — 26%
- Restricted Stock — 15%
- Profit-sharing/Gainsharing — 23%

Agree

- Stock Options — 53%
- Performance Shares — 33%
- Performance Units — 52%
- Annual Incentives — 43%
- SARs — 29%
- Restricted Stock — 44%
- Profit-sharing/Gainsharing — 35%

Source: 1990 The Hay Group "Survey of Compensation Committee Chairmen."

utive compensation proposals is internal, although the compensation committee plays a major role.

What all this seems to mean is that if a company wants superior executive talent, it has to pay what the market says such talent is worth and always link executive compensation as closely as it can to creating shareholder value.

Shareholder value means many things. Enhancing short-term financial results are important, and existing vehicles incorporate the right measures to improve these results. This supports the statistical results presented in Chapter 3.

This study also indicates you can't con the chairman. Executives understand well the value and effectiveness of various vehicles, and the chairman's compensation committee will not be bashful in proposing change.

Changes are coming, but slowly, say our 1990 Hay Group survey respondents to a general question regarding concerns or goals for the future of executive compensation. Representative quotes from the three areas most frequently addressed by executive compensation plans reflect this feeling. The third most common area covers fairness and equity, and typical comments were: "Growing disparity between executive and non-executive compensation is a major concern" and "equity among employees: no excessive compensation for top executives." The second most common was the link to shareholders and strategy, and the remarks included: "Stimulate a shareholder perspective in . . . decisions" and "Couple behavior with the long-term interests of shareholders." The most important area is still attracting and retaining top talent: "Attract and retain quality talent from a sadly diminishing pool" and "Attract and retain outstanding executive talent; this will be the competitive variable of the '90s."

Reconciling these potentially conflicting goals and concerns will be a challenge, but one that must be met.

In short, the current corporate governance process has been ineffective because the relationship between the board of directors and management relative to the board and shareholders is out of balance. I believe that, in response, shareholders will use corporate governance in the 1990s as the mechanism to challenge executive pay. Thus, we can expect intense pressure for change in today's corporate governance process.

CEOs have had principal responsibility for developing executive compensation plans. Shareholders have until now been silent on executive pay issues due to limited disclosure, limited oversight authority, and the ability to use the capital markets to monitor executive performance during the 1980s. Boards, which may or may not be independent of the company's management, have had the difficult job of reviewing executive compensation issues faced with intense management participation and interest on one hand and shareholder indifference on the other.

Given this situation, can corporate governance serve as the catalyst for changing executive compensation? I believe corporate governance can become an important mechanism in this effort. But the challenges will be great. First, it will be very important that in the midst of shareholder activism, boards of directors do not lose sight of the need for CEOs to be effective leaders. Today's investors are trying to signal that even good top executives are hired help, not royalty. To send that signal clearly, executive compensation must be administered with more control. That happens only if the board is linked closely to both the real ownership interests and to operations, so that it applies this direction confidently and credibly.

Board compensation committees must structure executive compensation programs so that they attract top management by providing competitive near-term rewards. The committee also must focus on the long term, because companies cannot be well managed if there is constant management turnover. Managers need strong long-term incentives that will encourage them to focus on business continuity. The challenge for the board is to balance the competing interests of shareholders and executives. It is important that increased board or shareholder scrutiny does not become so intrusive that it discourages the CEO from taking the strong leadership role that shareholders want. Thus, the board will face its greatest challenge in managing to increase the effectiveness of corporate oversight without quashing CEO leadership. "The ultimate test of a director's effectiveness, then, may be how successfully he or she can strike a balance between monitoring and meddling," wrote Thomas Dunfee in *Business & Its Legal Environment*.

As shareholders seek greater involvement in corporate governance, another challenge is that they must themselves organize; leadership is needed. This position has been assumed by the largest public employee pension funds.

Several entities seeking to galvanize shareholders on corporate governance are also providing direction. Two of these organizations, Institutional Shareholders Services, Inc. and the Counsel of Institutional Investors, Inc., target institutional investors. In organizing to influence management, shareholders need to recognize that they must have clear objectives, and they must have more than a fleeting commitment to the stock.

Corporate governance can be made more effective and does not need to be fundamentally changed. The success of this effort will be heavily influenced by the nature of shareholder and SEC interventions. But what can be done to make corporate governance effective? One underlying theme here is that the SEC does not need to mandate oversight, but that more voluntary corporate disclosure can level the playing field. With more information available, shareholders will be able to encourage boards to make needed changes voluntarily. I have already discussed the background behind current corporate governance structure. Let's explore the background to the current disclosure rules and the changing environment the SEC faces on this issue.

CHANGING DISCLOSURE NEEDS

The heart of American securities regulation has always been the spirit of full and fair disclosure. The fundamental purpose of disclosure has always been, and continues to be, to create "informed" buyers of a company's stock. In 1934, when the disclosure rules were developed, the SEC correctly realized that too much information can be almost as harmful as too little; it tried to require that only a manageable amount of information was to be disclosed. The commission based its decisions about what types of information should be disclosed on the nature of the investor community of the 1930s. Over the years, the information needs of shareholders and the external business environment have changed dramatically.

These fundamental changes require us to rethink disclosure completely from the standpoint of the investment community of the 1990s. Central to this thinking should be a reexamination of four guiding principles that have served us reasonably well in the past but that are now outmoded.

1. *Protection from Information Overload.* The amount of information available on issues, the speed with which it can be accessed, and the inexpensive portable equipment used to handle it have increased dramatically in just the last decade. The growth of a global economy, the advance of information technology, and simply the accelerated pace of events add further pressure to shareholder information wants. In the current environment, basic data overload is a constant fact of life, but information technology is readily available not only to manage data, but to organize and analyze them.

All this means that the information about executive compensation (among other topics) that investors want has expanded greatly. This desire does not solely reflect our current expanded ability to process information. It also reflects the greater importance shareholders attach today to the role executive compensation has in making and keeping a business organization competitive.

2. *The Unsophisticated Individual Investor.* We still operate from the 1950s model of Aunt Jane. Individual investors are as important to consider as ever, but we should recognize that

today Aunt Jane has a laptop with a modem and is buying into option spreads. The individual investor of the 1990s is capable of absorbing greater levels of disclosure information.

3. *The Sophisticated Institutional Investor.* We still assume that institutions can largely take care of themselves with respect to understanding executive compensation information. In fact, the complexity of numerous types of compensation vehicles has made it increasingly difficult to understand executive pay. While institutional investors are often skilled financial analysts, they do not have more than a cursory knowledge of executive compensation vehicles or how to properly value them. Thus, more disclosure is needed in this area for institutions.

4. *Proprietary Nature of Executive Compensation.* Executive compensation has acquired a protected status similar to trade secrets, as if disclosing senior executive compensation were tantamount to revealing proprietary data. The disclosure of information has been closer to what the company would tell competitors than what it should be telling owners. Companies have sometimes rationalized this as protecting a proprietary advantage, but that is not very plausible if one knows the extent to which companies survey each other's practices in this area.

I have shown that current disclosure rules reflect a 1930s investor community guided by principles that were valid once but are now outmoded. As the environment has changed, the disclosure rules must also change. Improvements in role definition and increases in disclosure can revitalize our corporate governance structure.

This is not to say that shareholders should circumvent the board or be actively involved in company operations. This is the board's responsibility. Involving shareholders in corporate micromanagement, whether pay programs or any other area, is difficult; it demands too much from a group whose interests are valid but may not be in the best position to make specific compensation decisions.

Shareholders can be more effective in challenging executive compensation by monitoring the board's performance and actively participating in the election of board members. Increased disclosure will help shareholders review the board's performance by providing them with essential information from which to draw conclusions. A good board is the key, and shareholder activism should concentrate on insuring the company has one.

Of course, all this is easier said than done. Here are six specific recommendations:

1. *Strengthen the board's independence on executive compensation matters.* Several steps will go a long way in this regard.

- Separate the position of board chairman from that of chief executive officer.
- Define "outside" director status to exclude employees, retired employees, relatives, or anyone with a significant economic relationship with the company.
- Define the qualifications for board membership and communicate them to the shareholders.
- Disclose detailed background information about potential board candidates and distribute it to shareholders at annual meetings.
- Have compensation consultants work under the joint direction of the board and management.
- Limit executive compensation review and membership on the compensation committee to outside directors so there is no direct link to the company.

2. *Rethink the concept of performance.* Performance measures should be based on achievement against agreed-upon goals and strategies developed by the board and the CEO. The outside directors should periodically evaluate the CEO's performance on these criteria.

Historically, companies have looked at the competitive

market mostly in terms of outcomes: levels and types of compensation at other companies. They have often looked at the performance dimension of compensation in only a superficial way. In the 1990s, compensation committees need to be hypersensitive to good compensation practices. They should take a broad but thorough perspective of their fiduciary responsibilities. Outside compensation specialists can provide direction with statistics and advice, but outsiders cannot relieve the compensation committee of its fiduciary responsibility. What corporations need is an adequate pay-for-performance rating system that measures executives on how well they execute agreed-on strategies for obtaining risk-adjusted excess returns. An organization must have a set of goals that is rational from the shareholder viewpoint, is stable enough to serve as a framework for planning, and is communicated broadly through its management. Performance management systems that measure progress toward the goals, allow targets to be set regularly, and are not too complicated to understand and administer must be designed. Performance expectations can be reinforced through compensation by understanding the degree to which the measurement scale is compressed by the selection process as we go up the organizational ladder, and allowing for that in the pay structure.

3. *Increase and improve proxy disclosure on executive pay.* The SEC's rules for proxy disclosure suggests that executive pay information was intended to be accessible to the shareholders and the public. While proxies do report executive pay data, the format and restrictions make the current data largely unusable. Even more damaging to the corporation, investors may believe the executives are grossly overpaid simply because they cannot interpret the proxy information. The following changes would help all parties in this area:

- Discuss the company's compensation philosophy and include the desired competitive position and the

mix of fixed and variable compensation elements.
- Describe all the applicable remuneration elements including the types of incentive vehicles the company is using.
- Provide a single table that reports separated *and* aggregated values for all remuneration elements (base, bonus, and other compensation such as insurance premiums).
- Develop a uniform valuation methodology to calculate present values of all compensation payouts.
- Report actual payouts that correspond to the performance cycle rather than reporting W-2 figures that are not correlated to the performance period.
- Present historical compensation data and performance trends so that shareholders can see compensation movement relative to performance trends.

4. *Encourage (but do not mandate) the use of shareholder proposals.* Subjecting all the various executive compensation issues to shareholder vote would not be in the best interests of the corporation or the shareholders. Shareholders should, however, be able to submit proposals to the board. These can signal the board that it needs to be more responsive to shareholder needs. Shareholders who want superior returns must set objectives that the board can steer by, and they should be willing and able to name new directors if they feel the board isn't doing its job.

5. *Retain a broad directional role for the SEC rather than direct intervention.* Government intervention is premature at this time. The commission's role is to define the boundaries of the playing field and to level it when that is clearly in the interests of corporate democracy. Changes in the rules appear to be necessary to reflect the changed environment, but they should be approached carefully and with an open mind. The current situation in corporate governance, and any problems it may have, came about not from bad rules but through

shareholder indifference. New rules can make it easier for individual and institutional shareholders to exert influence, but new rules cannot make them exert it. Ultimately, the amount of change that occurs will reflect the extent to which investors want to have influence—and the jury is still out on that. To the extent that the commission makes rule changes predicated on future changes in investor attitudes, it may be introducing costs that do not produce corresponding shareholder benefits.

The first changes should therefore cover broad issues that affect all or most companies. The SEC can level the playing field through increased disclosure. An improved playing field may be all the system requires to correct itself. If it does not, the SEC can then consider further changes.

6. *Pay part or all of the directors' fees in stock*. This will link the board's interests directly to shareholders.

As we will see in Chapter 7, the best of the new executive compensation techniques attempt to provide incentives for sustained increases in shareholder value. The emerging pattern of executive incentives has four distinctive features:

1. Participation is based on demonstrated value-added, not historical notions of what a position should receive.
2. Executive stock ownership is the primary objective of long-term incentives.
3. Downside ownership risk is featured very prominently.
4. Upside ownership opportunity corresponds to increased risk and is calibrated against criteria of improving shareholder's stake.

While executive compensation may be the focal point in the battle for corporate governance, it is only the beginning. For example, CalPERS (California Public Employees Retirement System), the nation's largest public-employee pension fund, has recently submitted shareholder resolutions calling for formation of shareholder advisory committees at several large public companies.

Companies without any shareholders or that have very few (for example, quasi-governmental and private companies), with little or no public market to tie executive compensation to, are not completely immune to the challenge. A number of companies have tried going private to insulate themselves from shareholder pressures. But they have found there is always a vested interest and ultimately someone either is, or acts like, the shareholder. If there is bank debt, the lender acts like a shareholder. If the employees own the firm, those who do not have large management roles behave as nonemployee shareholders would.

This issue will be prominent on corporate agendas for the next several years. Rather than being something to hide from, it is important that the United States tackles and solves this issue. We often hear that the answer to our problems is to be more like some other country (critics often use Japan and Sweden as models). But the real answer is to develop an American approach to today's corporate ownership realities—an approach that will work in a heterogeneous, pluralistic society with a strong anti-authoritarian tradition. The emergence of capitalism coincided with America's emergence as an economic power in 1850, and American capitalism has undergone several changes since. The time has come for one more.

CHAPTER 6

TAX, ACCOUNTING, AND LEGAL CONSIDERATIONS

They have no lawyers among them, for they consider them as a sort of people whose profession it is to disguise matters.
—SIR THOMAS MORE, *Utopia*

SIR THOMAS More said it well. What a world this would be without lawyers. Just imagine a world without legalese—clarity and simplicity instead of confusion and complexity. We could read our mortgages and understand what they said.*

Let's not forget the accountants. They want respect for their profession, which would appear to be directly related to the understandability of accounting principles: the less understandable, the more respect. So the accountants came up with complicated financial rules that no one outside the brotherhood understands.

In this chapter I will attempt to bring some understanding to this massive legal and accounting intervention in the otherwise routine subject of executive compensation.

I want to emphasize one point: While no one should ignore tax and accounting rules, they should not drive incentive compensation plans. As I have pointed out, incentive plans need to be motivational, and what and how they motivate

* I want to thank Rod Robinson for his invaluable contribution to this chapter.

should be their primary focus. Tax and accounting rules should simply be one more consideration in plan design.

How Compensation Plans Are Taxed

A major consideration for executives and the companies they work for is compensation's tax treatment. Executives want to know if it is taxable (of course it is), and if so, when? The company wants to know if the compensation is deductible (usually), and if so, when? The basic rule of thumb is that executives must pay income tax on amounts they receive as compensation in the year that they receive the reward. As a corollary, companies can usually take a compensation deduction in the same year.

This all seems simple enough, and indeed it is. But for the intervention of lawyers and accountants, this lesson in taxation would be over. Not content with this state of affairs, and spurred on by their professional advisers, executives wanted compensation today and taxation tomorrow. The whole idea was to get it, but somehow make it look as if it had not yet arrived. As a result, companies developed all sorts of deferred compensation arrangements to postpone the date of taxation.

The Internal Revenue Service saw all that was happening, and it was not amused. After all, executives were playing with the federal government's money. Consequently, the IRS developed two related, but distinct, doctrines to catch those individuals and make them pay their taxes when everyone else did: constructive receipt and economic benefit.

Constructive receipt. Under this doctrine, individuals may be taxed for income they do not actually possess if they have constructively or effectively received it. Basically, the IRS says that if a company makes money available to an executive by crediting it to his or her account or by setting it aside so that he or she can draw on it at any time, the executive is in constructive receipt and the money is currently taxable.

What does that mean? Well, taxpayers and the IRS disagree. Unfortunately for the IRS, most courts have tended to agree with the taxpayers. Perhaps the best way to understand the doctrine is to look at a few examples.

The easy case is where an individual agrees to defer compensation for a definite period before performing the services. An example is the boxer who, on the afternoon of an evening fight, agrees to defer a portion of his purse—before he earns it—at least one tax year into the future. Even the IRS agrees that this is all right. At the other end of the spectrum is the situation where the individual has already earned the compensation and the organization is ready to pay, but it gives the individual a choice of whether to accept immediate payment or to defer it. There would be little argument in the tax courts that this is constructive receipt. Deferral would be a poor choice here, because the individual would not have the funds available to pay the tax due.

What about a bonus situation, where the services have already been started, but the income has not yet been earned? For example, an executive is to be paid a bonus based on the company's operating income. The IRS maintains that in this situation, an election to defer the bonus after the services have started results in constructive receipt. Fortunately, the courts have consistently disagreed. In this situation, courts have allowed the executive to defer the taxes, because the total bonus amount to be paid is unknown, and it cannot be determined until the executive completes the services and it is possible to calculate the final operating income.

Taking this example a step further, what if the services have been completed, and then the executive elects to defer the bonus? We know what the IRS thinks—hand over those tax dollars, *now*. If the company has not determined the actual amount to be paid, however, the courts have held that this is not a constructive receipt situation. The courts regularly have been more lenient than the IRS would like in applying the constructive receipt doctrine. But the IRS keeps trying.

Actually, it is in the IRS's best interest not to push for immediate taxation; it loses money by doing so. Here's how. Let's assume an executive has $10,000 of compensation. If he is in the maximum 31 percent tax bracket, he has a $3,100 tax bill. The company, on the other hand, has a $10,000 tax deduction. At the corporate 34 percent tax rate, this translates into a $3,400 tax savings for the company. The government's net is actually a $300 revenue loss. If the executive defers the income, the IRS has use of the $300 during the deferral period. Without deferral, the government takes the loss immediately. Does the IRS know all this? Of course it does. Maybe it's what many people suspect—sometimes the IRS would rather be mean than smart.

Economic benefit. This is often confused with constructive receipt, but they are two distinct doctrines.

Under the economic benefit principle, an executive has taxable income whenever he or she has received an economic or financial benefit as compensation, whatever form it may take. The IRS often applies economic benefit in cases where an executive has not actually received property but can assign his or her interest in it. The IRS also uses it where an organization places property in trust for the executive without any substantial risk of forfeiture.

A good example of economic benefit is where an executive's deferred compensation is funded by an annuity (an investment contract guaranteeing regular payments for a fixed period or life), or it is placed in an irrevocable trust and the executive's interest is nonforfeitable. In these instances, even though the executive has not received the income (actually or constructively), he or she has received an economic benefit from it, because it is no longer at risk.

The economic benefit doctrine has essentially been codified in Section 83 of the Internal Revenue Code, at least concerning noncash compensation. Section 83 deals with transfers of property for services, such as an option or stock. The code often refers to this property as restricted property, because frequently there are restrictions on obtaining it.

The restriction, or risk of forfeiture, can be as simple as continued employment. For example, the corporation may transfer stock to an executive on the condition that he or she remain with the company for five years. During the five years, the stock cannot be transferred (sold). If the executive fails to satisfy the five-year requirement, the stock is forfeited. Because the stock is subject to forfeiture, the federal government does not tax the executive until the restrictions lapse. This is usually referred to as vesting. The company gets a compensation expense deduction (assuming it's reasonable, but that's another book) when the executive includes the property in income.

Basically, under Section 83, if an executive cannot transfer property, and it is subject to forfeiture, there has been no economic benefit and taxation is deferred until there is a benefit. As soon as the property is *either* transferable or no longer is subject to forfeiture, economic benefit is conferred, and the property is taxable income.

Of course the key question immediately becomes: How much taxable income? The fair market value at the time the property vests, less any amount paid for it, represents taxable income. For example, if the corporation gives an executive company stock with a fair market value at vesting of $20, the executive has $20 in taxable compensation income. But what about the fact that to get the stock the executive worked eighty-hour weeks, never saw the kids, and had to fight with the dog over sleeping space? Hasn't the executive actually paid something for the stock? Indeed he or she has, but the IRS does not think so. If the executive had paid $5 for the $20 stock, then he or she would only have $15 of taxable compensation income.

Suppose the corporation grants an executive some of this restricted stock but the manager does not want to wait until it vests to pay the tax. Can he or she pay the tax up front? Will the IRS permit someone to pay today, rather than wait and pay tomorrow? Of course it will. Just make what is referred to as a Section 83(b) election within thirty days of the grant and the tax can be paid.

Why would someone do this? Actually, at one time such an election could save many executives a substantial amount of tax. The key was the preferential capital gains tax treatment. A capital gain results when an individual sells property, such as stock, that has appreciated. Before the 1986 Tax Reform Act, the maximum tax on ordinary income (such as compensation) was 50 percent, while the maximum capital gains rate for property held one year was 20 percent, a very substantial difference. Obviously, if individuals could convert ordinary income to capital gains, they could enjoy significant tax savings. The Section 83(b) election was the way to do it. Here's how.

Assume that the corporation grants restricted stock to an executive when the fair market value is $10. The stock vests after five years. Assume also that the stock is worth $30 when it vests. Without a Section 83(b) election, taxation is deferred until vesting, in other words, when the stock is worth $30. At that point, the executive would have $30 that the IRS would tax as ordinary income. Before 1987, the maximum tax would have been $15 (50 percent). If, however, the executive had made an 83(b) election, the IRS would tax the grant at receipt—$10 and the executive would have paid $5 in tax (the same 50 percent). The additional $20 appreciation is taxed as capital gains. If the executive sold the stock at $30 when it vested, he or she would have had a $20 capital gain, and under the pre-1987 law, a $4 tax on the sale (20 percent of $20). With the Section 83(b) election, the total tax would be $9; without it, the tax is $15. Start putting zeros behind these numbers, and one can see why executives made this election.

The 83(b) election is not without risks. There is always the possibility the executive will leave the company before the stock vests. Or the value of the stock could decline significantly after paying the taxes but before vesting. In either case, the executive will have recognized ordinary income in the year of transfer but will have a capital loss in the year of forfeiture or sale. An 83(b) election gone bad is negative arbitrage.

Continuing tax reform has virtually eliminated the utility of Section 83(b). Now, with the differential between ordinary income and capital gains only 3 percent (31 percent versus 28 percent), most practitioners do not believe it is worth taking the chance of being taxed up front.

Our basic tax primer is completed. Let's look at what accountants have contributed to executive compensation.

How Accounting Rules Affect Executive Compensation

Often, the way financial accounting treats an executive compensation vehicle is a critical consideration in the type of plan a company adopts. In terms of a plan's impact on company earnings, the plans range from expensive to free. As we will soon see, there often seems to be little logic to the rules.

Three sources contain the primary accounting guidance for executive incentive compensation plans: Accounting Principles Board Opinion No. 25, "Accounting for Stock Issued to Employess"; Accounting Research Bulletin No. 43, "Compensation Involved in Stock Option and Stock Purchase Plans"; and Financial Accounting Standards Board Interpretation No. 28, "Accounting for Stock Appreciation Rights and Other Variable Stock Option or Award Plans."

Let's look at the treatment of stock, because the way everything else is treated derives from it. This whole area can be divided into several key concepts, and the first is the measurement date.

Measurement date. This is the date that the company determines the compensation expense amount. According to the literature, it is the first date on which both the number of shares to be issued and the price to be paid are known. For example, assume an executive is granted a stock option for 1,000 shares, with an exercise price of $20 a share (also its current fair market value), on January 1. On this date both the number of shares to be issued (1,000) and the price to be paid ($20) are known. So the amount of compensation cost is measured at that date.

We can apply the same principle to restricted stock. Assume instead that 1,000 shares of restricted stock with a fair market value of $20 are granted to an executive at no cost on January 1. The stock will vest after five years of employment. On January 1, both the number of shares to be issued (1,000) and the price to be paid ($0) are known, so that is the measurement date. But how do we know the 1,000 shares will be issued? The executive could leave after a year. Guess what? It does not matter. The accounting gurus have decided that if the only contingency on receiving the stock is continued employment, the accounting rules will not consider it. Even if the requirement to receive the shares were to be thirty years of continued employment, the measurement date is still the grant date.

Compensation amount. Measurement date was simple enough. Now we get into the compensation amount. The guides tell us that the compensation expense is the difference between the stock's fair market value on the measurement date and the amount the executive is to pay for it. Applying this to our stock option example, we have a $20 exercise price and a $20 fair market value on January 1. Thus, voilà! No compensation expense. Is it any wonder that companies love stock options? Essentially, the corporation gives away a part of itself, but the accountants say it does not cost anything. It does not matter that when the executive finally gets around to exercising the option, the stock will have appreciated. The only thing that matters is that there was no difference between the price to be paid (ultimately) and the fair market value of the stock on the measurement date.

The significance of this is shown by comparing the accounting expense with that for option profit. The figures in the chart below compare $10,000 in salary versus $10,000 in option profit.

While there is no accounting cost for these options, there is an economic cost and an impact on the balance sheet. Some experts say that if a cost is not measured, then it really is not managed either. This is one reason that some have said a cost should be associated with stock options.

Let's get back to restricted stock. Taking our same example: On the measurement date the fair market value was $20 and the price to be paid was $0. So the corporation has a $20,000 compensation expense. If the stock appreciated $10 during the vesting period, the executive would receive stock worth $30,000, but the company would still have only a $20,000 financial expense. Not as good as the stock option, where the expense was zero, but still not bad.

Performance criteria. But let's suppose we are going to make the executive's grant of options and restricted stock based upon future performance. After all, shareholders' interests should be served; if the corporation does well everyone does well, but if the performance is weak everyone suffers. There is an accounting problem with that approach. The accoun-

Implications of Salary versus Option Profit

Impact on	$10,000 Salary	$10,000 Option Profit
Company Accounting Profit	$10,000 Charge	No Charge
Company Taxable Income	$10,000 Deduction	$10,000 Deduction
Executive Taxable Income	$10,000 Income	$10,000 Income

tants prefer that executives not have to meet performance criteria to earn their options and restricted stock. Just take a look at this.

Suppose the same option for 1,000 shares was granted at an exercise price of $20. But now the company tells the executive that he or she has to perform to earn those shares. To be able to exercise, company stock price must rise $5 (similar to plans implemented by American Airlines and General Dynamics, among others). That does not sound bad. But the accountants say that on the grant date the company does not know how many shares it will be issuing because it does not know whether the stock will actually rise or not. The number could be 1,000 shares or it could be zero. Because the company does not know if the stock price will ever reach $25, it does not have a measurement date. When does it have a measurement date? When the stock's price hits $25; at that point it knows the shares can be issued. But look at what's happened: On the measurement date the fair market value is $25 while the exercise price is still $20. That $5 difference (or $5,000 on the 1,000 shares) is compensation expense, charged against the company's earnings.

This should not be considered just an academic exercise. I am aware of one major company that took this approach, and senior management was somewhat shocked to find that they had generated tens of millions in accounting charges.

There are ways to get around the accounting problems if a company desires a performance target. Basically it can achieve the same result, without a charge to earnings, by granting the option at a premium above the current fair market value. For example, if the fair market value of the stock at grant is $20, the company can set the exercise price at $25. Recognizing the higher exercise price, the corporation could grant more options. Two thousand shares exercisable at $25 produces the same profit as 1,000 shares at $20, if the stock rises to $30. (The arithmetic looks like this: $1,000 \times (30 - 20) = 2,000 \times (30 - 25) = 10,000$.)

Back to restricted stock. Let's say that the corporation

grants the executive 1,000 shares of $20 stock that will vest if the share price reaches $30 (a little tougher goal, but after all, it is actual stock and not an option on stock). Again, the financial accounting rules postpone the measurement date until the stock reaches this goal. At that time the company's compensation expense is $30,000 ($30,000 fair market value less $0 cost), which is charged against company earnings. The obvious lesson is that it is better to give the stock away than to make the executives earn it through some performance measure because any appreciation is charged against earnings.

Date of charge to earnings. That was fairly understandable, even though not necessarily logical. The last concept to learn is *when* the compensation expense is charged to company earnings. The principle is that a company should charge compensation expense to earnings for the related period of service. In most cases this will be the vesting period. For example, where restricted stock vests after three years, the expense is charged over the three-year period. The accounting charges on a $30,000 restricted stock grant vesting after three years looks like this:

	Charge to Earnings
Year 1	$10,000
Year 2	10,000
Year 3	10,000
Total	$30,000

While that example is childishly simple, this whole concept can get particularly murky when an organization includes performance contingencies. In that case, the company must make estimates (based on likelihood of achieving the goals) on a quarterly basis, and charge to earnings. Depending on the performance measures, and the likelihood of achieving them, the charge can go up or down each quarter. This can be extremely complicated, and it is exacerbated by the fact that the accounting rules provide virtually no guidance on it. It's no wonder that the simple option and restricted stock plans predominate; nearly everyone can understand them.

The Financial Accounting Standards Board (FASB) is currently reconsidering the accounting for stock compensation. This has been an on-again, off-again project since 1984. At this writing, it is likely there will be a change.

Now that we understand the legal and accounting principles, it's time to tackle the securities laws.

HOW THE SECURITIES LAWS AFFECT EXECUTIVE COMPENSATION

Securities law can be incredibly complicated, even in a seemingly small area like executive compensation. I will attempt to highlight only some of the issues. There are basically three areas on which I will focus: disclosure, registration, and short-swing profit liability.

Disclosure. Publicly held companies must disclose executive officer compensation in their proxy statements. This is basically to put shareholders on notice as to how much compensation the officers receive and what forms the compensation takes. The underlying idea is to give shareholders the necessary information they need to make an informed judgment whether the organization is properly spending their money to compensate the executives running the company. The disclosures cover general information concerning the compensation plan's operation, how the corporation determines the recipients under the plan, and any recent material amendments to the plan. The proxy statement must also disclose various pieces of information regarding benefits that executives received under the plan during the company's preceding fiscal year. The law requires more expanded disclosure if shareholders are voting to approve the plan or any amendment to it.

Unfortunately, proxy disclosure has seldom been a model of clarity. Counsel has been very resourceful at disguising compensation and even, occasionally, hiding it. Currently, Congress is reexamining the whole issue of adequate proxy disclosure.

If a corporation wants its securities listed on a stock exchange, stockholder approval of compensation plans may be required as a condition. In some cases, stockholder approval may not be necessary if awards are small and if the company grants them to an individual as an inducement to entering into employment. Stockholder approval may also not be necessary if substantially all employees participate in the plan. We discussed potential changes to disclosure more fully in Chapter 5.

Registration. The Securities and Exchange Act of 1933 generally requires an organization to register any offer or sale of a security. Registration is basically the filing of certain forms with the Securities and Exchange Commission to let it and the public know about new securities being issued. The question that arises with executive compensation is this: When does the grant of an award involve a sale? Generally, if an employee does not pay cash or other property in exchange for the grant of an award, it is not considered a sale of a security. On the other hand, many of the newer plans require executives to purchase stock via salary reduction, and these constitute purchases of securities and generally require registration.

Even if an offer or a sale is involved, several exemptions from registration may be applicable. Two of the more useful exemptions are for a limited number of employees participating or for a small amount of stock involved. For example, up to thirty-five employees has been used as a rule of thumb for the "private placement" exemption. Another provision allows an exemption every twelve months for up to $1.5 million in stock.

A company must also consider state securities laws. However, under most states' laws, registration is fairly simple, particularly if the company has already registered with the Securities and Exchange Commission.

Short-swing profit liability. Also called insider trading, this is the issue that gets everyone's attention. Under Section 16(b) of the Securities and Exchange Act of 1934, officers, directors, and beneficial owners of 10 percent or more of a company's securities ("insiders") must return to the company any profit realized from any combination of purchase and sale or sale and purchase of the company's equity securities within any six-month period. Transactions related to the distribution of stock or other securities under a compensation plan can be matched with unrelated (open market) transactions in the company's stock. Also, some transactions may be viewed as simultaneous purchases and sales in violation of Section 16(b). For example, a stock grant coupled with the withholding of a portion of the shares to satisfy an employee's tax withholding obligation may be treated as a simultaneous purchase and sale.

Many embarrassed (and angry) executives have had to return profits to their companies because of confusion over the rule's operation. There have even been cases of spouses of insiders buying and selling stock and having to replace the profit. To illustrate the dangers: Assume a company grants an executive an option for 1,000 shares at $30 ($30,000) on January 1, 1992. On March 1, the executive's spouse sells 1,000 shares at $35,000 on the open market. In certain situations, the executive will be deemed to have made a profit of $5,000, which must be returned to the company. If instead, the executive's spouse had waited until July to sell the 1,000 shares, there would be no short-swing profit violation (assuming no other transactions occurred).

One major thorn for insiders used to be that the *exercise* of an option was deemed to be a *purchase*. This meant that option stock had to be held for six months to avoid potential liability. The new Section 16 rules that became effective May 1, 1991, reversed this position so that the SEC no longer deems option exercises to be purchases. This means that insiders can exercise and sell their stock immediately, just as other employees can, as long as there has been at least six months between the date of grant and the date of sale. Since most options are granted subject to at least one year of vesting before they can be exercised, this is not a burdensome requirement (see the example below). It is too early to tell to what extent insiders will take advantage of the new rule. Immediate sales by insiders may be tempered by shareholders' desires to see executives own substantial equity positions.

APPLICATION TO OTHER TYPES OF PLANS

In this basic tax and accounting primer I have looked at stock options and restricted stock. Now let's take a look at a few other compensation vehicles. Some of these are fairly common, and others are at the cutting edge, and we describe them more fully in Chapter 7.

Stock appreciation rights may be a dinosaur because of the recently adopted amendments to the securities rules. As I pointed out in Chapter 2, SARs provide an executive with the option spread (the difference between the option price and share price at time of exercise) in cash or stock or both. The most common type of SAR is one issued in tandem with

The Relationship Between Grant and Sale Dates

1/1/91	6/1/91	1/1/92
Option grant	Earliest sale date of option stock (subject to vesting)	Stock options vest; executive can exercise and sell

a stock option. This means that an executive can exercise either the stock option or the related SAR. A few companies adopted SARs in addition to stock options. This is really generous, because when the executive exercises the option, it automatically exercises the SAR also—a kind of double hit for the executive.

The tax treatment follows that of an option. The government taxes the executive on the cash or stock payments when they are received. The company receives a compensation expense deduction equal to the amount the executive includes in income.

The accounting treatment is what is known as variable or "mark-to-market," accounting. Basically, this means that unlike a typical stock option, the company does not determine the compensation cost at the time of the grant. Instead, any stock price appreciation is charged to the company's earnings quarterly. At the date of exercise, the cost is fixed. This makes SARs very expensive for the company relative to options. An informal survey of companies shows that 90 percent of employees sell their stock immediately after the exercise of their stock options. Since this essentially converts a stock option into an SAR, the accounting difference seems rather arbitrary.

Corporations originally adopted SARs to provide money to executives so that they could purchase other options and pay any taxes associated with an option's exercise. SARs have been limited primarily to executive officers subject to the SEC short-swing trading rules. Now that executive officers can exercise options and sell the stock immediately, SARs are no longer necessary, and I expect their use to diminish.

Purchase and deposit options are designed to give executives additional motivation to increase the company's share price (I discuss these plans in more detail in Chapter 7). With both, instead of simply being granted an option, the executive pays for it. The difference between the two is that the purchase option payment is not refundable (that is, credited to the purchase), while the deposit option premium is refundable if the executive stays with the company but never exercises the option.

The tax treatment follows a normal stock option. Upon exercise, the taxable income is the difference between the market value of the stock and the exercise price, less the amount paid up front. For example, assume that the executive pays $2 up front for an option with an exercise price of $10. If the executive exercises when the share price is $15, he or she has taxable income of $3 ($15 minus $10 minus $2). The company receives a compensation expense deduction equal to the amount the executive includes in income.

As long as the exercise price is equal to the fair market value of the stock at the time of grant, then normal option accounting applies, and there is no charge to earnings. If the FASB should ultimately decide on a charge to earnings for stock options, these purchase plans will go a long way to reduce or eliminate any possible charge to earnings.

Premium options are options granted with the exercise price above the stock's current market value. Like its purchase and deposit cousins, a premium stock option gives executives additional incentive to raise share price.

The tax treatment is exactly the same as that of a regular option. The executive is taxed on the difference between the stock price and the exercise price when the option is exercised. The company receives a tax deduction equal to the amount the executive includes in income.

The accounting treatment is also the same as a regular option—no accounting charge as long as the premium exercise price is constant over the exercise period.

A restricted stock/stock option combination plan is designed to get executives to hold on to their option stock after they exercise by sweetening the deal. Basically, restricted stock is granted in conjunction with the exercise of an option. For example, a company may grant one share of restricted stock for every five option shares when the executive exercises the options. The restricted stock, however, vests only if the executive holds the option stock for three years or more.

Like a traditional option, the spread between the exercise price and the market value at exercise is taxable income. The executive is taxed on the value of the restricted stock when it vests, unless he or she makes a Section 83(b) election (an unlikely event). The company receives compensation expense deductions in the year of exercise and again when the restricted stock vests.

The accounting is the normal stock option and restricted stock accounting. There is no charge to earnings for the stock option. There is a charge equal to the value of the restricted stock at grant.

Earned restricted stock is a slight variant of restricted stock with a performance requirement. The typical performance restricted stock would vest as the company meets various performance targets. Under this version, vesting does not begin until after the company achieves its performance goals. For example, an executive earns 20 percent of a restricted stock award for every 20 percent increase in share price from the price on the award date. The executive earns the total award when the share price doubles. The earned stock then vests after five years of continued employment. This provides additional incentive to raise the share price.

This has the expected tax treatment. The executive is taxed on the value of the restricted stock when it vests, assuming no Section 83(b) election. The company receives its compensation expense deduction in the year of vesting.

Remember that this is just a variant of performance restricted stock, so the compensation cost is *not* fixed at grant. Instead, the charge on each earned 20 percent will be equal to the value of the stock when the executive earns it. This amount will then be prorated over the vesting period. The accounting expense from this plan would be greater than traditional restricted stock.

Reload stock options is a compensation vehicle that everyone keeps telling us is designed to encourage stock ownership. I am not so sure it accomplishes its intended purpose. Nevertheless, reloads are getting much attention.

Under a reload plan, when an executive exercises his or her option by trading in already owned stock (a stock-for-stock exercise), he or she receives a new option at the current market price for the same number of shares that were traded in. The goal is to put the executive on equal footing with executives that use cash to exercise. For example, in a stock-for-stock exercise, if an executive exercises an option for 1,000 shares with an exercise price of $10 ($10,000) when the current market price is $40, he or she will deliver 250 shares and receive 1,000 option shares, for a net increase of 750 shares. If the executive immediately sold these 750 shares, he or she would realize the $30,000 profit inherent in the option. If instead, the executive used cash to exercise, he or she would pay $10,000 and receive 1,000 shares. If the executive then sold these shares, he or she would then realize the same $30,000 profit (the $40,000 sale price less $10,000 paid to exercise).

If the executive sells the stock immediately, it doesn't really matter if he or she uses stock-for-stock or a cash exercise; the profit is the same. But if the executive holds the stock for appreciation, it could make a big difference. Assume the market price rises from $40 to $50 in a year. After the stock-for-stock purchase, the executive could sell the 750 new shares for a $37,500 profit. If the executive used a cash exercise, the 1,000 new shares could be sold for a $40,000 profit (the $50,000 sale price less $10,000 paid to exercise). The reload makes up for this difference by granting the executive an option for 250 shares at $40. One year later, when the market price is $50, the executive would realize the same $2,500 additional profit he or she would have enjoyed if he or she had exercised with cash. A pretty good deal for the executive.

Normal taxation rules apply to the exercise of the option. As for the reload, there is no taxable event when the company grants it. When the executive exercises the reload option, it gets normal option taxation—the spread between the option price and the market value is taxable income. The company receives a compensation expense deduction in the year the executive exercises the option.

Normal option accounting applies to both the original option and the reload, so there is no charge to earnings.

The tax, accounting, and legal aspects of executive compensation can be very complex. Both corporations and their executives should seek professional legal and accounting advice from specialists in the field to avoid the worst pitfalls.

With the perspectives of the financial takeover specialists, the executives, the institutional shareholders, the lawyers, the accountants, and the tax specialists behind us, we can finally pose some solutions.

CHAPTER 7

SOLUTIONS TO THE EXECUTIVE COMPENSATION CRISIS

*I expect CEOs and senior managers to adopt
many of the organizational practices of private
owners as a way to make their companies more
efficient.*

—MICHAEL JENSEN

NOT LONG ago, the CEO of a financial services company, under pressure from his parent corporation, came to us. The company had major financial management and human resource problems.

Until the mid 1980s, the company had been private and for more than 20 years had enjoyed high profit margins. Indeed, it had been so successful that a larger corporation, not in the financial services business, bought it. The acquisition, which transformed the executives from owners to employees, changed the corporate culture dramatically, and as the 1980s evolved, the firm's profits grew thinner and thinner, ultimately turning into large losses. Morale deteriorated, and the firm was finding it harder to retain productive people or to attract the professionals it needed.

The parent had set three fundamental goals for the subsidiary's program:

1. *Conserve cash.* The money the company was paying in annual bonuses did not appear to be doing much good either

in motivating people or in retaining them. Yet every time management attempted to discuss cash compensation or annual bonuses, the firm verged on being torn apart, a situation not dissimilar to the one at Lehman Brothers in the early 1980s.

2. *Enlist the employees in the common cause.* Top management wanted to bring back the partnership culture the company had enjoyed when it had been private. This was a challenge, because real ownership was no longer available to the employees.

3. *Take pressure off the annual incentive process.* The parent company was putting tremendous pressure on the subsidiary's management to increase profitability and to stop paying huge bonuses at a time of poor financial performance. Management wanted a closer bond between the employees and the company's future achievements. It wanted to devise a way that the employees had as much—or more—at stake on a long-term deferred basis as they did on an annual, or cash compensation, basis. If it were possible, management wanted to make the employees feel that they were owners of the company and to get them to take more prudent risks with the company's capital.

After we analyzed the situation, we designed a phantom partnership plan, which was not incremental to the cash compensation but substituted for part of it. Employees buy into the partnership through their annual incentive. While their actual annual cash compensation is less than what it would have been, the difference goes into the phantom partnership. The value of the partnership shares in five or seven years will depend upon how well the company performs over the years.

As an example, take an executive who has a $200,000 salary and who in a normal year would earn a $300,000 cash bonus. Under the phantom partnership plan, he or she has the same salary, but receives a $200,000 cash bonus and has $100,000 go into the phantom partnership. This amount has the potential to sink to zero, or to grow to as much as $300,000 or $400,000 over a five-year period. So at any given time, the employees may have an amount greater than the annual cash bonus at stake.

Employees who leave before vesting in three or four years lose the money they deferred that went into the plan and any appreciation. The benefits are taxed the year paid, and the company has a tax deduction that year in an amount equal to the amount it pays to the employees. There is accounting expense, but it is spread over the vesting period.

The plan therefore motivates the managers to take appropriate risks. Not too much, because they have real downside risk and their partnership value could actually fall below what they paid, but enough risk so that they end up generating a decent return. And the potential returns on the investment can be impressive if the firm's financial performance even begins to approach the historical levels; the employees could earn 500 or 1,000 percent on their investment. They think twice about leaving and are highly motivated to invest for the long term rather than for the short, for the company as well as for themselves.

While the company's CEO and the parent corporation's senior executives embraced the plan, the employees were very unhappy with it initially. Although the money going into the plan was not coming directly out of their pockets, they felt as if it were. To overcome the resistance, we gave many presentations and prepared extensive pro forma financial sheets. There was a lot of grumbling, but the company installed the plan more than two years ago. While it's impossible to call the plan an unqualified success at this writing, it certainly appears to be pushing the company in the right direction. Between the improving general performance of all financial service firms in the company's market segment and the increased teamwork and motivation I believe the plan encourages, the company's results have improved dramatically—from a significant loss in the year the plan was implemented to a respectable profit currently. The grumbling has stopped. The defections have slowed, turnover has improved, and recruiting has become easier. The company appears to be getting the returns it should be, given the financial performance of the industry as a whole.

In five years, of course, the plan is scheduled to begin paying out, and the company will then have another problem as these situations always do, but then the firm will probably establish another plan. The company is, in fact, considering establishing a rolling plan, a new plan every year, so that no matter when an employee arrives, he or she would be part of the program, and no matter when he or she leaves, he or she would leave some money on the table.

HOW TO ENCOURAGE THE PROPER OUTCOME

The solution to the executive compensation crisis has been implied throughout the book. The challenge is to maintain or strengthen the link between pay and performance and to ensure that compensation plans encourage the proper outcome—increasing shareholder value. A public corporation accomplishes this by creating a different motivational atmosphere. Such a culture generates compensation and financial strategies that replicate and integrate the best aspects of the corporate and the management buyout (MBO) worlds.

Consistent with the theory that ownership creates different types of management behaviors, Steven Kaplan in a University of Chicago Working Paper found that management buyouts have significant increases in operating income and cash flow. They also experience increases in market value 77 percent greater than the general market experiences over a comparable period. While Kaplan's study does not specifically mention them, it is almost universally accepted that MBOs rarely make acquisitions. This could be because they are trying to conserve cash, but I believe that since the managers are risking their own capital, they do not want to play the highly risky—that is, low probability of high return—acquisition game.

John Kitching, writing in the *Harvard Business Review*, reported that in the LBOs (leveraged buyouts) he studied, managers put in an average of 25 percent of their net worth. Revenues grew dramatically after the buyout. Earnings before interest and taxes (EBIT—the best measure of profit in a highly leveraged transaction) did fall short of budget for the first years, but dramatically exceeded previous performance. Employment remained stable, meaning that operating efficiencies created the improved performance, not layoffs.

Can a culture that contains both traditional corporate and LBO styles yield very high pay levels? Yes, but only if the shareholders do well also. Given the downside risk these executives will have, perhaps the world will accept their pay levels. Will these plans yield different corporate and financial strategies? Yes, and these strategies, which will involve fewer or lower-priced acquisitions, should more closely match shareholder concerns.

Many companies, financial takeover specialists, and management buyouts have already shown the way public corporations, their shareholders, and executives may benefit dramatically. While the American public corporation in its current format may have been "eclipsed" by highly leveraged transactions, there are still steps available to salvage the corporate form. These changes contain enough differences to resolve many of the form's fundamental conflicts, such as the goal of some companies to grow through acquisitions despite the uncertain, and often negative, impact on shareholder value.

The public corporation's other problems include too little debt, too much splintered equity, too little cash flow moving into positive net present value projects, too little cash distributed to the shareholders, and too many acquisitions for the wrong reasons (like growth or diversification at too high a premium). The solution combines elements from the best ideas from corporate finance and executive compensation:

- Increase debt.
- Reduce equity.
- Compensate management and the board heavily in stock. Require management to buy and hold significant amounts of stock.
- Eliminate stock options in their most popular form.
- Modify all annual and long-term cash compensation programs to connect them to value-creation measures, such as return on assets or cash flow, instead of accounting measures, such as net income or return on equity.
- Create phantom or simulated equity plans at the subsidiary or division level that unite compensation levels to economic value creation.

The increasing-debt, reducing-equity pattern has already begun, showing up at the macroeconomic level, where huge amounts of debt have replaced equity for the entire economy (see Figure 7-1). Obviously, too much debt is unacceptable also—for example, Resorts International and Federated Department Stores. Yet many companies remain underleveraged.

While a program that incorporates all these elements would be ideal, any plan that approaches it would be a major improvement over the current combination of accounting-based programs and stock option plans. Even if the accounting-based programs survive, introducing an ownership element into them would motivate executives to create economic value.

The accounting programs are acceptable for annual plans, as long as the company adds a longer-term incentive that creates shareholder value. The goal is to put the CEO and the senior executives in the position of balancing their short-term gain against the long-term potential. In this situation, the executives will make a positive net present value investment that may hurt their annual incentive, but is presumably the

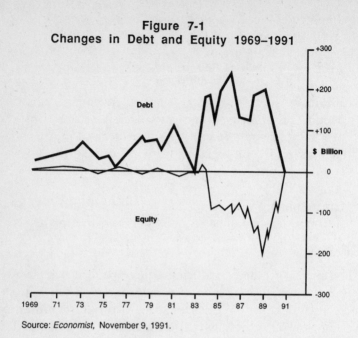

Figure 7-1
Changes in Debt and Equity 1969–1991

Source: *Economist,* November 9, 1991.

right decision because the executives act with a shareholder's perspective.

Accounting-based incentive programs that promote net profits or return on equity and stock option plans have been the basis for executive and management incentive efforts for more than two decades. They worked well when the economy grew rapidly; accounting measures correlated fairly well with cash flow and stock prices rose, thereby masking the missing downside risk in stock options. Many risky strategies motivated by stock options "paid off" thanks to the U.S. economy's underlying growth from 1981 to 1989 rather than their inherent wisdom. In today's uncertain economic environment, these programs may no longer create economic value because the stock market will not continue to pay higher and higher prices. Today, these programs will motivate flawed strategies, particularly in the area of corporate acquisitions. The time for new programs and new concepts has arrived.

THE EXECUTIVE COMPENSATION AUDIT

How can a company tell if its compensation plans are both motivating and supporting shareholder objectives?

The real test of executive compensation is how well it motivates and retains an organization's top talent and how well it provides rewards commensurate with results, plus how well it unites executive and shareholder goals. In today's highly competitive environment, motivating executives is critical, not only to a company's day-to-day performance but also to its ability to move into the future. Companies must ensure that their plans—as generous as they may appear to be—are really helping to retain their key executives and motivating them to achieve overall business and performance objectives. Are executive pay policies and practices, in fact, linked to broader goals and shareholder objectives?

Companies must address key concerns related to the structure, strengths, and weaknesses of executive pay plans and answer important design questions. The issues include:

- Eligibility
- Incentive mix
- Plan administration
- Performance objective and targeting
- Mix of corporate, division, and individual objectives
- Competitors' markets
- Timing of grants/payouts
- Payout format (cash or stock)
- Deferrals
- Building and retaining executive ownership
- Effectiveness of communications programs

These elements combine to form a general perspective of a compensation package's effectiveness.

Companies must examine their executive incentive plans to determine if they are actually achieving their business and compensation objectives. The following symptoms suggest a weak executive compensation program or one that needs review:

1. Lack of long-term perspective among the senior executives
2. Unsuccessful divestiture/acquisition programs
3. Takeover threats
4. Employee stock allocations at or near a "ceiling" (for example, 5 percent of shares outstanding)
5. "Underwater" options or restricted stock
6. Strategic decentralization
7. Major executive turnover
8. Difficulty in recruiting
9. Poor financial/stock performance
10. Low market-to-book value
11. Below-industry earnings growth
12. Lack of teamwork among senior managers

To address these issues, answers to the following questions are needed.

1. What positions or people truly influence long-term performance?
2. What key measures relate directly to the strategic plan or to shareholder value?
3. How difficult is it to move the performance level beyond target?
4. What do the competitive data show about payout ratios? What ratio is needed to change behavior here?
5. Should performance measures, weights, ratios, or leverage differ for corporate staff and line managers?

6. How should designs differ for corporate and subsidiary positions? Should the sum of the subsidiary performance measures add up to the corporate measure?

7. What should the timing be for measures, grants, plans, earnings, and payouts? Does timing reflect business and recruiting cycles?

8. Should payouts be in cash or stock?

9. Should additional deferrals be allowed?

10. How should the plan be communicated? Who should administer it? What happens when an employee retires? Quits? Is fired?

11. Does a plan require shareholder approval? Compensation committee approval?

An audit also helps determine if the right vehicles for executive compensation are in place. Different factors regarding the company have different implications for the ideal vehicle (see table on next page).

The next task is to design a program that balances risk properly and incorporates the above issues.

A NEW PHILOSOPHY OF RISK BALANCE

Since most companies have stock option plans, any audit—and ultimate changes—must start with a review of options.

As I've said, the fundamental problem with stock options is their asymmetric risk profile—the shareholders have upside opportunities and downside dangers while the executives have only the upside. The goal should be to create upside benefits *and* downside risk for the executives as well transferring some risk from the shareholders to the executives, without alienating the executives and without simply giving the executives large stock grants.

While not insurmountable, this is not a trivial task. It requires planning, some courage, and an executive group pre-

Choosing the Right Executive Compensation Vehicle

Factor	Issue	Vehicle of Choice
Public vs. Private Company	Are reported earnings important?	Stock options
Taxpayer Status	Are significant corporate tax deductions important?	Stock options (nonqualified); restricted stock
Shareholder vs. Other Measures	Is creating shareholder value a top priority?	Stock-based plans with "purchase" component
Stock Options— Tax Rates	Are capital gains taxed favorably relative to ordinary income?	Incentive stock options
Shares Allocated to Plans	Have 5 percent of shares been distributed to employees?	Stock purchase plans / Cash plans
Earnings/Stock Price	Are earnings relatively volatile?	Full value plans / Restricted stock

pared to invest for the long term and to share some risks with the shareholders. It may even require a somewhat different personality type than the typical historical American corporate executive.

In the past, American executives had to be good at operating issues; however, given the nature of the large companies for which they worked, they also had to be good at internal politics, bureaucratic administration, and the gamesmanship involved with negotiating favorable budgets because their incentive plans were based on them. These internal negotiations are common in large companies, and at the end of the day, with senior management's approval and the board of directors' imprimatur, the company eventually sets realistic budgets. But this negotiating skill per se is an important one.

The shareholder value plans I'm suggesting, where executive and shareholder interests are linked, reduce the games-manship because the concept of an empire-building budget is no longer relevant. The executive owns part of the company, and it is in his or her interest to increase the company's value, and to do so without undertaking excessive risk. This implies that someone who is good at corporate politics or at internal negotiations would no longer be effective because the new focal point will be on customers, on competitors, on quality, on customer satisfaction—all the things associated with the creation of shareholder value.

So while it's an overused and hackneyed word, the concept of the entrepreneur is a real one. These executives will act like owners, going for maximum shareholder value within the constraints of the balance sheet. Their focal point will be on the external world, not on the internal. In the long term, and perhaps even in the short term, it is in the interests of every-one affiliated with the public corporation, the board of di-rectors, shareholders, employees, customers, vendors, and even the executives, to have such compensation plans. Ex-ecutives will change their behavior and they will make better strategic decisions—including (or especially) acquisitions—so that the firm's long-term survival and prosperity will be en-hanced. If this is true, and I think it is, executives ought to embrace these programs.

A key supposition here, of course, is that executives can have a positive influence on their company's stock price by making managerial decisions that improve the company's financial performance and that the stock market ultimately rewards. Executives have told me, on the other hand, that they are reluctant to be paid primarily or heavily or even a little bit on stock price performance because they don't in-fluence it. They don't want to be subject to the "vagaries" of the stock market.

Yet their shareholders are subject to these vagaries. Their shareholders' wealth is influenced by how well the stock per-forms, and many, many studies demonstrate that companies with a better franchise, better quality, better customer service, better and more innovative products perform better in the stock market than companies with poor financial performance, poor products, and poor service. This after all is how stock analysts, stock brokers, and investment bankers make their living—by the empirically verified phenomenon that well-managed companies perform successfully over a long period of time.

True, over a short period, it may be disadvantageous to the executives to have a high ratio of stock to cash compensation, because, for whatever reasons, the stock market undervalues the stock. Nevertheless, a strong relationship between financial performance and stock price exists. Executives will be rewarded proportionately for making good decisions that have superior financial results.

From the executive's viewpoint, of course, it is bully to get rich whether the company thrives or not. Whether this was ever truly possible in the past is unclear. It is certainly true that, given the scrutiny of the media, of the Congress, of the SEC, of institutional shareholder groups, and of institutional investors themselves, no major publicly traded company will have such a "heads I win, tails I win" compensation strategy available in the future. At least partly as a response to an assault by shareholder activists, ITT, for example, changed its executive compensation programs in 1991. ITT's program moved from a "discretionary" to a formula-based plan, one combining stock price and return on equity. According to Gilbert Fuchsberg in the *Wall Street Journal,* under the new plan, ITT is to issue options at a price at least as high as the stock's fair market value at the time of the grant, and, to exercise them, the executives have to wait until ITT's stock price has risen at least 25 percent or until the year in which the options expire. The revised bonus plan is to pay cash bonuses based on return on equity, and each of ITT's nine operating companies has separate ROE targets under the plan.

How a corporation implements these plans determines whether executives find them to be motivating. If the company executes them properly, the plans can be effective; if not, not. The corporation can address this challenge in a number of ways.

1. The company should begin encouraging—or requiring—managers to hold stock early in their careers so that by the time they become senior executives they hold large amounts.

2. The firm should allow the stock purchase through various types of loans, perhaps even "forgivable" loans if the executive achieves certain objectives.

3. The company should permit an executive to purchase stock with pre-tax dollars. This tax-leveraging technique can be very powerful, and it is a major source of purchasing power and of course available only to employees.

4. The company must build large upside potential into its programs to offset the introduction of downside risk. It can design these new plans with the same economic cost to the company and same economic value to the executive as the old plans now have on a present value risk-adjusted basis. Examples of these are "purchase" stock options or executive stock purchase. Large upside potential can be very attractive to an executive's entrepreneurial spirit.

5. The corporation should design phantom stock plans for the subsidiary or division level.

I will return to these issues in some detail as I describe some of the new plans. I must address another issue before I do so, however.

How Much Stock Is Enough?

It is extremely difficult and expensive for many CEOs to own a significant percentage of their company's stock. To own 2 percent of the stock of a company with a $4 billion market value, for example, requires an investment of $80 million, far beyond the means of all but a handful of CEOs, despite their million-dollar cash compensations. This is one drawback to being a huge corporation.

Is there a rule of thumb that boards of directors can use to determine whether the CEO owns enough stock to influence behavior and performance? Based on my consulting experience, the following ratio is useful:

$$\frac{\text{Value of Stock Owned}}{\text{Current Cash Compensation}}$$

In other words, if the CEO owns $700,000 in stock and current cash compensation is $200,000, his or her ratio is 3.5 to 1—too low, I feel, to influence behavior. If the ratio lies between 5 and 10 to 1, the CEO has sufficient real compensation "at risk" to change behavior. This means in practice that if the stock price increases by 10 percent in a given year, the executive has doubled his compensation, even though half of that increase would be on paper. Conversely, if the stock price drops by 10 percent, compensation would be zero. For example, assume an executive has $10 million worth of stock and receives a $1 million cash compensation. If the share price drops 10 percent, the executive will have suffered a $1 million loss in the stock's value. That offsets the cash compensation, so he or she would in effect earn nothing from the company that year. This appears to be sufficient risk-sharing between the executive and the shareholders. Naturally, the industry, the phase of the business cycle, the CEO's tenure, and the stock price volatility influence such a ratio.

I recommend that companies develop a similar ratio to compare stock options to stock owned. A corporation can reduce many stock option problems if the executive owns a sizable amount of stock in addition to options. Significant stock ownership allows the company to continue granting options without being afraid the CEO will embark on a course of excessively risky strategies. The ratio would be:

$$\frac{\text{Number of Stock Options}}{\text{Number of Shares Owned}}$$

Based on the ratios calculated in Chapter 4 and my consulting experience, I recommend that this be no higher than 3 to 1. This means that a dollar increase in the stock price yields a four-dollar increase in compensation (a dollar from the stock and three dollars from the options). Conversely, a dollar decline in stock price yields a dollar loss only from the real shares. This 4 to 1 payoff ratio should be sufficient to motivate appropriate risks without being excessive.

How Early Stock Purchase Can Add Up

The easiest and probably the least painful way to combine shareholder and executive interests is to encourage the executives to buy and hold stock starting early in their careers. If these employees become executives they will already own significant amounts of stock. Such a program has the added advantage of having all employees, whether they become senior executives or not, holding large amounts of stock. Many studies have shown—among them, those by the National Council of Employee Ownership—that companies in which the employees own large amounts of stock perform significantly better than those in which the employees do not.

Such a program would require that employees at all income levels buy a certain amount of stock each year, for example 5 percent per year at low income levels, rising to 15 percent at very high income levels. These purchases could be at the market price or at some type of discount. Obviously, such a plan would directly serve the shareholders' interests, although some might argue that a discount would be unfair because it is not available to the ordinary shareholder. Other employee compensation plans could be structured to pay for the discount, however; the company could reduce the retirement plan, for example, to reflect the discount, thereby keeping the plan's total cost constant.

A number of vehicles currently available under the tax code encourage such stock purchase. These include Employee Stock Ownership Plans (ESOP), a stock alternative inside the standard 401(k), broad-based employee stock option plans (Apple Computer, Pfizer, Du Pont, Pepsico, and Merck have these), and Employee Stock Purchase Plans (Section 423 of the tax code). The last is a very attractive plan that surprisingly few companies use. The plan's favorable feature is that an employee can buy as much as $25,000 worth of company stock per year at a 15 percent discount from the fair market value. In other words, a loophole in the accounting rules allows the corporation to sell the employee up to $28,750 worth of stock for $25,000—in effect, giving $3,750 extra income to the employee—and not take it as an accounting expense.

The table on page 201 presents the results of a prototypical plan that requires employees to buy stock annually and hold it. The results are dramatic. By the time an employee rises through the ranks to become CEO he or she will own stock worth $644,589, almost twice the cash compensation. This could be in addition to any stock purchased through stock option plans. While that total remains below the level sophisticated shareholders would like their CEO to own, it is well above typical levels, and it puts the employee into a good position to participate in a CEO-level stock-based incentive program.

Since most companies do not have this type of early stock purchase programs, companies need alternative vehicles. Ideally, these would have some aspects of the historical plans,

How Stock Purchases Add Up over the Years

	Annual Income			Percent of Income Used to Buy Stock	

	Annual Income	Percent of Income Used to Buy Stock
	Below $50K	0%
	$50K–$75K	5
	$75K–$100K	7
	$100K–$150K	9
	$150K–$300K	10
	Above $300K	15

Year	Compen-sation	Stock Purchase This Year	Number of Shares Purchased	Stock Price	Total Number of Shares Owned	Value of Total Shares at Current Price
1	$ 50,000	$ 2,500 (5%)	50	$ 50	50	$ 2,500
2	54,500	2,725 (5%)	52	53	102	5,350
3	59,405	2,970 (5%)	54	55	156	8,588
4	64,751	3,238 (5%)	56	58	212	12,255
5	70,579	3,529 (5%)	58	61	270	16,396
6	76,931	5,385 (7%)	84	64	354	22,601
7	83,855	5,870 (7%)	88	67	442	29,601
8	91,402	6,398 (7%)	91	70	533	37,480
9	99,628	6,974 (7%)	94	74	627	46,327
10	108,595	8,967 (9%)	116	78	743	57,610
11	118,368	9,774 (9%)	120	81	863	70,264
12	129,021	10,653 (9%)	125	86	987	84,431
13	140,633	11,612 (9%)	129	90	1,117	100,264
14	153,290	15,329 (10%)	163	94	1,279	120,606
15	167,086	16,709 (10%)	169	99	1,448	143,345
16	182,124	18,212 (10%)	175	104	1,623	168,725
17	198,515	19,852 (10%)	182	109	1,805	197,013
18	216,382	21,638 (10%)	189	115	1,994	228,502
19	235,856	23,586 (10%)	196	120	2,190	263,512
20	257,083	25,708 (10%)	203	126	2,393	302,396
21	280,221	28,022 (10%)	211	133	2,605	345,538
22	305,440	45,816 (15%)	329	139	2,934	408,631
23	332,930	49,940 (15%)	341	146	3,275	479,002
24	362,894	54,434 (15%)	354	154	3,629	557,386
25	395,554	59,333 (15%)	368	161	3,997	644,589
26 Becomes CEO						
Total/Average	$169,402	$459,172	3,997	$ 95	3,997	$644,589

Assumptions:
1. 9 percent increase in compensation each year (reflects increases and promotions).
2. Twenty-five-year tenure when promoted to top executive.
3. Initial stock price of $50 increases by 5 percent per year.

while going much further to link executive and shareholder interests. The philosophy behind an early stock purchase program implies that young CEOs own significantly less stock than older CEOs. If relatively new CEOs were able to accumulate large amounts of stock on their own or through the exercise of options, a formal program might not be necessary. The data in the table on page 201 support this assumption.

Regardless of a CEO's age, it is in the shareholders' interests to have him or her own a large amount of stock. The next two sections explore vehicles—purchase stock options and purchase restricted stock—that accomplish this.

How Purchase Stock Options Operate

In 1979, when the Chrysler Corporation was on the verge of bankruptcy, Lee Iacocca as CEO set a bold new precedent for his and other companies. He took a salary cut to $1 a year and in exchange received an incentive program based on stock price appreciation. Iacocca in effect "bought" stock options. His risk-reward profile was very similar, if not identical, to the profile of his shareholders, many of whom had lost significant value as Chrysler's stock had fallen over the years. Iacocca and his executive team made dramatic changes to the company that paid off as Chrysler returned from the brink. Was the risk associated with changes in the business strategy exactly the same as the risk the shareholders desired?

This is, of course, impossible to tell. Chrysler's strategy

CEO Age and Stock Ownershp

CEO Group	Median Age	Median Value of Stock Ownedl
10 youngest	39 years	$6.3 million
10 oldest	76.5 years	$171.7 million

SOURCE: Forbes, May 27, 1991.

was, as they say in football, a "blocking and tackling" approach—that is, the firm worked on the fundamentals of the automobile business: designing and manufacturing better cars, reducing costs, emphasizing customer service, and advertising aggressively. The strategy did not include a major diversification campaign implemented through acquisitions.

While Chrysler has its problems today, the company's financial and stock market performance improved dramatically in the decade after this highly unusual compensation plan, and Iacocca received large profits on his stock. From the edge of bankruptcy, with a stock price below $2 and a negative cash flow, the company improved impressively. The stock rose to $20 per share by 1985 with significant cash flow and profits of more than $1 billion. How different would the outcome have been if Iacocca had received a large cash compensation package in addition to numerous stock options? Such a package would have eliminated Iacocca's downside risk, and the behavioral implications could have been profound. The probability of value-reducing acquisitions would have been high.

Here was an attempt—apparently initiated by the executive himself—to align the shareholders' interests more closely with those of the CEO. Using the diagram in Figure 7-2 of the asymmetric risk profiles of shareholders and executive stock option holders, we can see how such a purchase stock option changes the profiles. The shaded area to the left of the "breakeven" line reflects such a program's added downside risk. While the shareholders still have a higher level of downside risk potential, I believe that the added risk to the executive is sufficient to change behavior significantly. Executives, as I said earlier, need not have an identical profile to the shareholders to act in their interests. Given the other hazards to which the executives are exposed—from losing an annual bonus to actually losing the job—adding a modest amount of downside risk to their stock program should be sufficient to create the desired behavioral change.

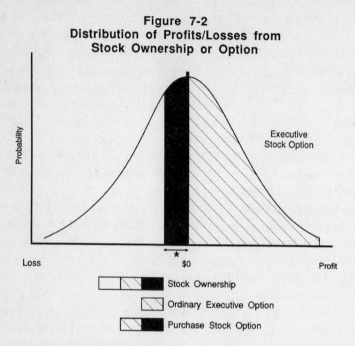

Figure 7-2
Distribution of Profits/Losses from
Stock Ownership or Option

*Reflects purchase price paid for stock option.

Some have argued that stock options fill the role of motivating risk-averse executives to undertake the appropriately
risky strategies the shareholders actually want. These same
people argue that the lack of downside exposure is appropriate since executives cannot diversify their market risk (since
they primarily own one company) as an outside shareholder
can do by buying the shares of several companies. This point
has some merit; however, the executive shareholder has in-
finitely more control over the company's financial performance than does the outside investor, since the executive
makes the operating decisions. In the final analysis, the ap-

propriateness or excessiveness of the risk motivated by options is an empirical or statistical matter. That is, what is the measurable outcome? The data presented in Chapter 4 yield a clear answer: excessive risk.

Figure 7-2 shows the modified risk profile from a purchase stock option that would address this issue. Obviously, if the executives were required or encouraged to purchase shares of stock outright (as they are in a management buyout—an MBO), then they *are* outside shareholders and their risk profiles move from being similar to being identical to the profile of all shareholders.

A stock option, as I've said, gives the holder the right (but not the obligation) to purchase the underlying stock at a fixed price within a given time period. As a security, it has value— and depending upon the circumstances, extraordinary value. Options on stock—called calls and warrants—are available for many companies. Any outside investor can buy these on the open market, including the New York Stock Exchange, the American Stock Exchange, and the Chicago Board of Options Exchange. These securities have some features in common with executive stock options but also many differences. The table on page 206 shows the similarities and differences.

As the table shows, there are some critical differences. One key difference is number 6: Outsiders always pay for their options, executives rarely do. A key similarity is number 14: Executives and outside option holders do not generally end up owning the shares of the company's stock. Since this is the explicit purpose of executive options, it is a distinct failure of the current design of these plans.

I have asked directors of compensation at dozens of companies whether executives who exercise their options hold the stock. Perhaps one executive in ten holds it. While the executives may have sound financial reasons for doing this, it is *not* in the interests of the shareholders to have it occur. In fact many companies have specific programs—called "cash-

"Outside" versus "Executive" Stock Options

Feature	"Outside" Stock Option	"Executive" Stock Option
1. Right to buy stock	Yes	Yes
2. Obligation to buy stock	No	No
3. Fixed price	Yes	Yes
4. Fixed time period to exercise	Yes	Yes
5. Option itself has value	Yes	Yes
6. Investor/employee pays for the option	Always	Rarely
7. "Strike" price* equal to current market price	Not necessarily	Usually†
8. Typical time period to exercise	6 months	10 years
9. Exact value determined by an external market	Yes	No
10. Value can be determined by mathematical models	Precisely	Approximately—controversial valuation methods
11. Option itself can be sold (liquidity)	Yes	No
12. Designed for leveraged play on stock price	Yes	No
13. Options are intended to create stock ownership	No	Yes
14. Options generally create stock ownership	No	No

* The strike price of an option is the exercise price; that is, the price the owner must pay for the underlying shares if he or she wishes to take ownership. A publicly traded call option with a strike price *below* the market price sells for a much higher price than one with the strike price equal to the market price. This premium reflects the amount the option is "in the money."

† Most current executive option plans have a strike price equal to the actual price on the date of the grant. The historical practice of granting options with a discounted exercise price has been discontinued at most companies since they appear to be unfair to outside shareholders. Premium-priced options for executives are becoming more popular and I discuss them later.

less" exercise and "stock-for-stock" exercise—that allow and, by implication, encourage executives to receive the option's profit in cash or stock without holding on to the shares the option covered.

Here's an example of a cashless exercise. Assume 1,000 options with an exercise price of $20 and the current price to be $25. The intention of the option is to have the executive write a $20,000 check, receiving stock worth $25,000. If the executive does so, he or she has a $5,000 profit on the option ($25,000 − $20,000). However, cashless exercise replaces the traditional method for exercising options. Through a previously arranged "temporary loan" with an outside securities dealer, the executive exercises the 1,000 options and sells the 1,000 shares immediately. The executive takes the $5,000 profit in cash or stock—usually cash—and the company withholds the appropriate taxes.

As an aside, it is interesting to point out a conflict that may occur between an executive perquisite and shareholder interests. Many companies provide company-paid executive financial counseling. These counselors prudently encourage the executives to sell much or all of their stock to "diversify" their portfolios. This would occur, for example, after the exercise of stock options. While these sales may benefit the executives, they move counter to the shareholders, who want executives to own stock. I am aware of one large successful corporation that pays for counseling, and its executives own virtually no stock.

An option to buy stock is very valuable, whether for outside investors or an executive. Outside purchasers of options (for example, on the Chicago Board of Options Exchange) have a market to determine current value. They also utilize sophisticated mathematical models, for example, Black-Scholes, to estimate an option's value.

On average, a Black-Scholes calculation yields an executive option value of around 30 percent of the market price for an "at the money" option (strike price = market price) with "typical" price volatility, a 5 percent dividend, and ten years until expiration. This means that if the current stock price is $30, and the strike price of the option is also $30, then the option itself is worth around $9 (30 percent of $30). It is important to remember that when an outside investor exercises the option he or she must pay, in this example, the full $30 for the shares. The price the investor paid for the option ($9) is *not* credited toward the purchase price. Therefore the option's breakeven price is $39—which reflects the option's very high value.

Since the executive option holder does not typically pay for the option itself, he or she has received a very valuable right for "free."

Because executives do not typically pay for their options— remember that the Iacocca example was an unusual one that made business headlines—they have great difficulty valuing them, and in my experience they tend to undervalue them. Without an external market, options are difficult to value. It depends on the stock price, the strike price, the stock's dividend rate, the risk-free interest rate available on the open market, the time until expiration, and the stock's volatility. Most option pricing models, including Black–Scholes, incorporate these factors. The following table shows the impact of each.

Higher volatility increases an option's value because the odds increase that the stock price will rise above the option price. This is one reason why options motivate executives to undertake risky acquisitions. Acquisitions tend to make a company's stock price more volatile, which makes the executives' options more valuable. As I showed in Chapter 4, evidence exists that acquisitions often do intensify the volatility of the buying company's stock price.

Increasing the stock ownership, or funds at risk, will change executive behavior and ultimately improve the company's financial performance. The key to accomplish this, as I've said, is to create some downside risk, if not equivalent to then similar to the outside shareholders' risk. Since executives

Factors That Influence an Option's Value

Factor	Impact on the Value of an Option	Comment
Price of the Stock	Positive*	A 10 percent increase in a high-price stock means a larger dollar amount than a 10 percent increase in a low-price stock.
Strike (Exercise) Price	Negative†	The higher the strike price, the greater the stock price must increase for the option to have value.
Dividend Rate	Negative	A higher dividend means the company has less cash to invest to create stock price increases.
Risk-free Interest Rate	Positive	If the buyer borrows money to buy the stock (instead of the option), a higher interest rate increases the cost of borrowing. This makes the option more valuable.
Time until Expiration	Positive	The longer the time, the greater the likelihood the stock price will increase.
Volatility	Positive	The more volatile the price, the more likely the stock price will rise above the option price.

* "Positive" means an *increase* in the factor yields an *increase* in the value (price) of the option.
† "Negative" means an *increase* in the factor yields a decrease in the value.

previously received their incentive plans for no "consideration" other than employment, introducing a "purchase" feature could be unattractive unless the plan has other positive features.

Specifically, companies have granted executives incentive plans with a given risk-adjusted present value. Theoretically, the companies could allow a *larger* grant under the incentive plan, but because there is downside risk, the risk-adjusted present value could be identical or even higher. For example:

Alternative A: Current Plan—Ordinary Option

1,000 options at $50 current stock price granted for no consideration

Grant Value	1,000 × $50 = $50,000
Total Present Value	1,000 × $15 = $15,000

(See the Appendix for valuation methodology.)

Alternative B: Purchase Options

2,000 options "sold" for $5 each

Consideration	2,000 × $5 = $10,000
Grant Value	2,000 × $50 = $100,000
Total Present Value	2,000 × $15 = $30,000
Minus Consideration	− $10,000
"Net" Present Value	$20,000

Our present value methodology makes key assumptions about future stock price increases and represents a compensation opportunity. Which plan is ultimately more lucrative of course depends on the stock's price on the exercise date. I believe the second alternative will motivate the executives to undertake better strategies. In this sense, from the shareholder perspective, Alternative B is superior. It may also be superior for the executives. The table on page 211 shows the impact of varying stock prices on the two different plans.

Recently, the CEO of International Multifoods, a major food company located in Minneapolis, decided to purchase a large stock option package with his own capital. This executive waived $1 million in cash compensation over a five-year period in return for stock options of an equivalent value on a current value basis. In this case, the executive could purchase $1 million of stock options with a ten-year term for $200,000 per year, yielding $5 million in grant value of the options.

For example, if the CEO's total salary plus bonus for 1989

Option Profits for Different Plans

Stock Price at Exercise	PROFIT	
	Alternative A	*Alternative B*
$ 40	0	0
45	0	0
50	0	0
55	$ 5,000*	0†
60	10,000	$10,000
65	15,000	20,000
70	20,000	30,000
100	50,000	90,000

* ($55 − $50) × 1,000.

† ($55 − $50 − $5) × 2,000.

had been $500,000, the new incentive program entitled him to only $300,000 in cash. With the other $200,000, he would purchase options on 50,000 shares (assuming a market price of $20) each year, or 250,000 shares over the full five years. In this arrangement, the CEO has put his own money at risk. If the market price increases from $20 to only $24, the executive will be no better off than had he received the $1 million in cash in lieu of the $5 million in options. If the stock rises significantly, the CEO will be handsomely rewarded. If stock doubles to $40, for example, the CEO's $1 million investment will net him $4 million ($5 million in profit minus the $1 million cost). This is clearly an example of an incentive program that makes the executive face the risk of losing a significant sum at the same time that it offers the reward of a big payoff, thereby motivating him to increase shareholder value.

How Executive Stock Purchase Can Work

Another vehicle that can more closely link the investment interests of executives and outside shareholders is the purchase of restricted stock. With this mechanism, executives pay part or all of the fair market value of a restricted share. The same $50-per-share stock, for example, could cost the CEO $20 per share, a 60 percent discount. As the stock rises, the CEO receives a profit of $10 for every ten-point increase. At a market price of $70, the executive's profits are $50 per share. Because the corporation is selling the stock at a discount, it would not allow the executive to sell the stock for two or three years.

With the stock option purchase, the executive's wealth does not increase until the market price increases beyond the purchase price. With a restricted stock purchase, the executive's wealth is at risk only when the market value drops below the purchase price, in the example above, if it drops below $20, although he does have his capital invested. From the shareholder's point of view, purchased stock offers a more compelling reason for executives to focus on increasing shareholder value than does ordinary restricted stock, which is no more than a gift.

Either form of purchase is clearly preferable to the giveaway alternatives in terms of the incentive they provide to prevent the company's market value from sliding. Under traditional restricted stock plans, when the stock price drops to $30 from $50, shareholders lose $20 a share, executives with stock options lose nothing, and executives with restricted stock grants can still earn $30 a share. With a purchased stock option, the executive loses $5 a share, and with a purchased restricted stock, the profit is only $10 a share.

When taken to an extreme—even if the stock bottoms out at zero—in the purchased stock option and purchased restricted stock cases the shareholder is no longer the only party whose wealth diminishes significantly. Executives' profits with conventional options and restricted options stay at zero, while purchased options cost them $5 per share, and purchased restricted stock cost them $20 per share.

As these examples show, purchased restricted stock and

purchased options introduce an element of executive risk to stock-based incentives. Another way a board of directors may stimulate creating shareholder value through long-term incentives is by offering restricted stock in tandem with a stock option, but making the grant contingent upon the executive's holding stock obtained through the option for a specific period. Companies also use these arrangements to strengthen the bond between a company's stock price and the executive's financial well-being.

Company directors may want to consider other long-term incentive plans that use stock. These can be significantly more effective than the currently structured stock option plans. In addition to the purchase stock option and the executive stock purchase plans I have already discussed, there are three other approaches.

1. Buying stock with loans. One of the clearest ways to unite shareholders and executives would be to do a sort of management buyout without actually creating the financial and legal costs associated with a true buyout. The end result of a management buyout is that the executives own the company. They are working or employee shareholders. A company can do this on a more gradual basis, or with a lower percentage than a true management buyout in which the executives typically buy 30 or 40 or 50 percent of the stock. What I'm suggesting could be a much lower percentage that would still pick up a lot of the behavioral improvements that a management buyout offers.

One possibility is for the company to lend the executives money at a favorable interest rate to buy stock. The executive could not sell the stock for the period of the loan—say, anywhere from three to five years.

According to reporter Margaret Elliot writing in *Corporate Finance,* Henley Group's chairman Michael Dingman created such a plan. The Henley Group is made up of thirty-five businesses that Allied Signal had spun off as poorly performing. The managers bought 5 percent of the stock at a slight premium to market. Some $97 million of the $108 million purchase price of this 5 percent was financed with nonrecourse loans, with the executives putting up the other $11 million. A nonrecourse loan in this case means that the executives own the stock's value or the loan principal, whichever is less. These are very favorable terms, but reasonable since the executives were putting up real cash, which is very unusual in executive compensation circles. In this case, the executives have tremendous upside potential and real downside risk, more than enough, in my opinion, to create a highly motivated executive group, but one that will measure the risks and rewards of all strategies from the shareholders' perspective.

In another situation, the CSX Corporation loaned employees up to 95 percent of the purchase price of a significant amount of stock, which they bought from the company at the then fair market value. The loans have a term of five years, and the executives earn dividends on all the stock, which almost covers the interest on the loans. But the amount of the loan principal will be reduced by amounts related to the increase in the stock price so that, for example, if the stock goes up by $20, the loan principal is reduced by 25 percent, creating a 25 percent discount on the stock purchase price.

Another wrinkle on this would be to make the loans forgivable based on other operating results. This could make the plan much more palatable and attractive to the executives, so that, for example, if the company has an historic cash flow of $10 a share or an historic return on equity of 20 percent, the terms for forgiving the loan—that is, for reducing the loan principal—would be set so that if the company achieves a higher level of cash flow or a higher return on equity, it would reduce part or all of the loan. This would encourage the executives to be highly motivated to improve the company's financial performance and its economic value because they would be shareholders and have a long-term cash plan.

2. Restricted stock in lieu of bonus. I described this earlier as part of the General Motors strategy for conserving cash while creating employee shareholders. This is a very good plan, and it converts restricted stock from one of the less attractive compensation plans, in my opinion, to one of the more attractive. While General Motors paid 100 percent of the cash bonuses in the form of stock in 1989, restricted stock could be 25, 50, or 75 percent of the cash bonus. To be fair to the employees, the restrictions would probably be shorter than typical restricted stock—usually three to five years—because they have in this case paid for the stock. The company would restrict them from selling something they would have otherwise received or would have received in the past as cash.

Another possibility for making this plan attractive to employees is to convert the cash to stock at a discount. For example, say an employee would have received a $100,000 cash bonus; instead of realizing $50,000 in cash and $50,000 in stock, the executive receives $50,000 in cash and, say, $75,000 worth of stock restricted for two years. In effect, the employee is buying the stock at a discount.

3. Premium stock options. These have been growing more popular in the corporate world. A premium stock option is where the option's exercise, or strike price option, is above the fair market price on the date of the grant, so that if the stock is trading for $50 on the date of the grant, the exercise price is $60. Those who favor these options argue that the first amount of the gain in the stock price should belong to the shareholder and only gains above—in this case, $10—should create profit for the executives.

A famous example of premium stock options that I've already described is that of Steve Ross at Time Warner. The option price is $150, and when the options were granted the stock was selling for less than $110. While these premium options have some advantages over ordinary options in that they are less a guarantee of compensation than ordinary options, they also have some strategic problems. Based on the theory I've laid out in Chapters 3 and 4, the premium-priced option might motivate executives to take even more risk and to chance even riskier strategies because they have to work so hard to make the stock price rise and give their options value and because, as with ordinary options, they have no downside risk. Based on this theory, one might expect that Ross will undertake risky acquisitions based on his current stock ownership and stock option profile, including these premium options. Compared to standard stock options, however, premium options are probably a superior long-term incentive.

OTHER CREATIVE EXECUTIVE COMPENSATION PLANS

General Dynamics implemented a new compensation plan that meets some of the goals of the new type of compensation programs but, in my judgment, falls short in a critical component. The plan pays a cash bonus equal to 100 percent of base salary to the top twenty-five executives if the stock price rises from $25 to $35 a share, and an additional 200 percent if the stock price rises to $45. Importantly, the company changed its savings plan for all employees by changing the company contribution or matching component from a cash match to a stock-only match. This is important because it puts emphasis on the employees, not only on the executives. These plans do go a long way to link the interests of shareholders with the executives and the employees. This is significantly better than a long-term incentive plan based on accounting measures, such as annual profit or return on equity, which may or may not be associated with the creation of shareholder value. But in effect, the General Dynamics executive plan is really a stock appreciation rights plan, with the shareholders absorbing all the risk and the executives obtaining much of the gain. This is a major shortcoming, but at this writing the stock price has passed the $45 mark and the executives are eligible for their large bonuses, although the company may be backing away from part of the payments because of media and shareholder pressure. It is also critical to point out that, generous as these payments may be, the executives have received less than 2 percent of the total gain that the shareholders received.

At Chrysler Corporation, almost 2,000 top executives took a voluntary pay cut of up to 10 percent of their base salaries in July 1989, a plan the employees labeled "You Bet Your Check," according to Claudia H. Deutsch in *The New York Times*. The money went into an escrow account, and if Chrysler's costs dropped $1 billion by the end of 1990, the company would return double the money. If costs did not drop, the participants would lose everything. In fact, Chrysler did cut costs, and the managers received their checks.

LONG-TERM INCENTIVE PLANS AT INDEPENDENT DIVISIONS AND SUBSIDIARIES

Independent divisions and subsidiaries present special problems. They do not ordinarily have their own stock, and the parent's results may not reflect the subsidiary's performance. One major trend in executive compensation in the 1990s is the move to create long-term incentive plans at independent subsidiaries based on the subsidiary's performance.

This is a break from the past when executives at subsidiaries typically received stock options in the parent company's stock. This may have been appropriate given the organizational strategy that was prevalent at American companies in the early to mid-1980s. At that time, corporate headquarters possessed primary power at most major corporations. Relatively large corporate staffs—especially strategic planning departments—made the key decisions about investments, especially the allocation of capital and key acquisitions. The operating units, whether divisions or subsidiaries, were left with operating responsibility, primarily production, marketing, and sales.

A new organizational model has been developed recently, led by General Electric. This pattern pushes decision making, autonomy, and accountability down in the organization into the operating companies. Interestingly, European parents of American subsidiaries have embraced this organizational paradigm, having recognized the positive benefits of allowing their American employees to succeed based on their own accountability.

The compensation implications of this type of organizational change are obvious and profound. The compensation plans must support this new independence in the form of profit sharing and gain sharing plans for the broad base of employees, plus long-term incentive plans based on increasing the subsidiary's value. The benefits are clear: The executives will be highly motivated to improve their unit's operating performance, and therefore its economic value to the company as a whole or for itself if the unit is ever sold or spun off. These plans tend to be most effective when:

1. The subsidiary's product line differs from the parent company's.
2. A limited amount of interdivisional transfer of products exists. For example, crude oil and refined products in the petroleum industry create large amounts of transfers and might be unsuitable for separate plans.
3. The labor markets are different.
4. The business cycles are different.
5. The subsidiary is a relatively small part of the total company, less than, say, 10 percent.
6. The subsidiary may be sold.

Once management has decided to create a long-term incentive plan at a subsidiary, the next question is: What should the performance measure be? Should it be based on the parent company's stock price appreciation? If so, the company can use purchased stock options or the other vehicles I've described.

If management feels that the subsidiary or division is different enough that it should have its own performance measures, it would then want to devise some kind of a cash plan. This could be a performance unit plan, which would be based on the business's accounting or other operating measures. Or it could be a phantom stock plan where the parent comes up with an estimated value for the subsidiary; this could be based on an appraisal or on a multiple of revenue or profit. With a value established, the parent gives the subsidiary's executives some phantom shares—pretend shares in the subsidiary—and three, four, or five years later, reapplies the appraisal or formula; the executives are entitled to a percentage of the appreciation.

Presumably that works better than just giving the executives stock options in the parent company where they feel the subsidiary isn't large enough to make a difference, or if it has a different business cycle or product cycle, and so is not linked to the parent company's performance.

The key obstacle to these plans is with the parent company executives. Given the differences between the businesses, the subsidiary plan may well generate payouts to its executives at a time when the parent company's plans produce modest or no payouts. It takes a brave corporate CEO or a strong corporate culture to allow this to occur. The key question senior managers must ask themselves is: How risky is employment and success at the subsidiary? If the subsidiary's success is guaranteed, or if its key executives have guaranteed jobs back at the parent company if the subsidiary fails, there is no reason to create a different, let alone generous, long-term incentive plan at the subsidiary. Once again, if the plan's designers keep the different risk profiles in mind, they can often find the answer to otherwise intractable questions.

The key challenge in these plans is the same as the one at the corporate level: Who bears the risk? If the parent com-

pany bears all the risk, in this situation as the sole shareholder, then subsidiary executives may be motivated to
undertake more risk than the parent company truly desires.
Once again, corporations can address this agency conflict
problem by requiring the executives to purchase their long-
term incentive plan. Since subsidiaries usually have no stock
available themselves, the plan must be a long-term cash plan,
where the payouts are based on increases in the value of the
subsidiary. This would be a plan into which the executives
will buy. The example I described at the beginning of the
chapter, of the financial services subsidiary, is a purchase plan
at the subsidiary level.

With some creativity, long-term cash plans can be used to
replicate the best features of stock-based programs. Examples of companies that have been the exceptions include General Motors, which kept some stock for EDS, and Hughes
Aircraft. Litton Industries also sold stock in its Western Atlas
International subsidiary to its management.

In a situation I was involved with not long ago, the financial services parent company viewed its technology subsidiary as an investment, and may ultimately sell it. The
subsidiary's senior executives came to us because their parent
company's stock programs weren't working, and the executives were uncomfortable. The only long-term incentive
plan they had available was the parent's, but it was irrelevant
as far as the small, unrelated subsidiary was concerned. These
executives could grow the subsidiary, but if the parent company stock didn't do well, they wouldn't be rewarded for it.
The problem was to develop an incentive plan that would
link payouts to creation of value at the subsidiary level.

The key here was to create shareholder value, and we therefore used a valuation and appraisal approach. The vehicle of
choice in such a situation is a phantom stock option. This
means that the key employees share—via phantom stock options—in the increase in the subsidiary's appraised value. The
plan was structured to allow the executives to participate

financially if the parent company sold or spun off the subsidiary.

While I generally recommend that executives buy their options from existing cash compensation, in this case the executives' remuneration was well below the market. Therefore, I recommended that the phantom options close the gap between what these executives earned and what managers in comparable companies earned. This approach is superior to increasing salaries, since it increases opportunity rather than fixed compensation. This program had an additional "purchase" aspect; the participants had to relinquish participation in the parent's stock-based programs. For several positions this was a substantial "give up." Nonetheless, the key executives describe themselves as being able to act like owners under the new plan.

NONEQUITY PROGRAMS ON A GLOBAL SCALE

Another example of a nonequity incentive plan, as it was applied to U.S. subsidiary executives, illustrates the potential for corporate and shareholder benefit on a global scale. A foreign company with a portfolio of several U.S. firms wanted to refocus annual and long-term incentives and link payout and performance more closely. Management also saw a need for a cost-efficient evaluation of its total compensation program, including base salary, annual incentives, long-term incentives, and benefits.

After I reviewed management input and financial analyses from the firms it had acquired in the United States, I found a wide variation in annual incentive policies. Most long-term incentives were tied to each firm's results, a policy the firm deemed necessary to attract, motivate, and retain senior management within each unit. Because of the foreign parent's extremely volatile profitability and the potential benefits from cooperation among the units, some coupling to the parent company's financial results was desirable.

The plan's objective for the subsidiaries was to focus each firm's executives on the growth of their own units as well as on creating value for parent shareholders. The plan's underlying principle was that reward should be based on the performance of the entity in which the executive could influence long-term results. The long-term incentive plan sought to create wealth for the executive through the achivement of specified strategic objectives. Generating teamwork among the U.S. subsidiaries was an important plan byproduct.

After we thoroughly evaluated the alternatives, we recommended a plan that awarded phantom shares based on the value of each individual firm. The shares would be paid out 50 percent in cash and 50 percent in parent company stock options (based on a valuation formula). Phantom shares offered the parent company an opportunity to encourage executive long-term sustained performance, without dilution of earnings per share. An additional benefit for the parent's shareholders came from the ability to deduct the unit's cash layout as a compensation expense. Most important, the parent company maintained flexibility in designing share valuation formulas. Like the phantom shares, the options offered the company a tax deduction and further served to align the long-term interest of the executives and shareholders.

The benefits to the executives from the stock option component included the psychological advantages of real common stock ownership. The plan also provided the executives with significant opportunities for capital accumulation. The only risk involved for the executives was the possible downward stock price movement.

The parent company learned that to be effective, a long-term incentive plan of this type must limit eligibility to the key executives who are most accountable for establishing and achieving each unit's long-term strategy. Further, to achieve its incentive and retention objectives, the company should be highly selective in who participates. When a corporation allocates phantom shares, it must evaluate participant groups based on job responsibility to determine the phantom share grant levels and the long-term incentive award opportunity for each incumbent.

The award of phantom shares, based on the firm's growth, should be determined by a formula tied to revenues and operating margin. Similarly, the growth in the value of each participant's share account should be based on revenues and operating margin.

As this example illustrates, such a plan offers promising benefits for both a foreign parent and its subsidiary firm. Connecting the subsidiary executives' pay to their own performance as well as to that of the foreign parent offers a creative solution to an often complicated relationship. Subsidiary executives may have to educate the foreign parent's management about this type of long-term incentive plan, as there may be no precedent for it in the parent's culture. Demonstrating the link between pay and performance, as well as the plan's cost effectiveness, however, may be sufficient to enlighten the parent company about the plan's overall benefits.

The Unsuccessful Cases

I have been arguing that a sharing of risk between executives and shareholders is good for all parties—including the executives—and for the economy as a whole. Unfortunately, just as there are instances where a company's management ignores the laws of probability and is successful, so also are there cases where despite a highly motivated management that takes appropriate risks, companies do indeed enter hard times or fail. The most famous cases of failed leveraged buyouts are Dart and Revco.

I can only presume that some companies in some industries would experience financial distress and even bankruptcy under any circumstances, including higher employee ownership. Nevertheless, I am confident that there will be fewer such failures if management and all employees own more of the company.

There are of course examples of broad-based employee stock ownership that experienced financial distress, notably American West Airlines and Weirton Steel, previously one of the most successful ESOPs in history. An ESOP does not guarantee profitability or job security. As a United Steel-workers official said to *Business Week* reporter Maria Mallory about Weirton employees, "You just don't keep them on because they own the company, or there's not going to be any company to own." Which brings us to another important controversy.

In addition to the general criticism of executive pay during the 1990s, another more ethical issue has arisen. The criticism goes something like this: Why should CEOs get rich, either through stock options or any of the newer shareholder value plans, on the backs of the general employee population, employees who are suffering from layoffs and reduced compensation?

Among the companies at which this issue was raised are General Motors and Chrysler. At GM, the criticism was that the unionized work force was not getting its profit-sharing payouts (which were implemented earlier at the expense of a standard wage increase) at a time when management was receiving its bonuses and a retiring chairman was receiving a supplemental pension. At Chrysler, Lee Iacocca was receiving large amounts of compensation at a time of layoffs and no profit-sharing payouts.

At General Dynamics the top executives were eligible to receive payouts under the special incentive plan described above. Part of the stock price increases, it was argued, came from cost reductions based on layoffs and cutbacks.

At Time Warner executives were receiving large cash and stock compensation at a time of layoffs at Time, a virtually unprecedented event.

This is a highly complex issue, having emotional, economic, and even political overtones—and it may have been part of the motivation for some of the anti-executive compensation legislation under study in the Congress. This issue is directly linked to a broader issue about the social cost of improving competitiveness at American companies at a time of increasing competition from abroad. A November 1991 *Business Week* cover story captured the concept: "Tough Times, Tough Bosses: The New Breed of CEO in Corporate America."

While the article emphasized the layoffs side of this equation, the logic seems to apply to the executive compensation issue. Concerning layoffs, Norman Blake, the newly installed CEO of USFG, the large insurance company, seems to have summarized their strategic use best: "It's the lifeboat theory. The boat can't hold everyone, and not everyone is contributing to the boat's forward motion." In other words, the job security of the many is preserved by having a profitable, effectively run company.

Layoffs are devastating to the individuals involved, and they have a large social cost. The company's survival, however, and the jobs of the remaining employees may require the reductions. Interestingly, it frequently takes a new CEO—often participating in significantly leveraged incentive and stock-based plans—to make these difficult decisions: reducing staff, selling divisions, and cutting dividends. A new CEO does not have the strategic, emotional, or political ties to past policies and has more freedom both psychologically and from the board of directors to make unpopular decisions.

These tough new types include Lawrence Bossidy at Allied Signal, Michael Walsh at Tenneco, and Stanley Gault at Goodyear. It is essential to note that the stock market has supported them, increasing their corporations' stock prices shortly after they announced many of their moves. Also, many of the newest CEOs in large American companies tend to be in troubled industries: cars, trucks, auto parts, tires, metals, mining, publishing, and broadcasting. This is yet another example of the relatively effective working of the stock market where boards replace the CEOs of poorly performing companies.

Executive compensation is an equally sensitive issue. Should chief executive officers—new or old—get rich by implementing these plans? The only realistic answer may be that there is no other alternative. It takes money to motivate an individual to undertake unpopular business decisions. No executive in my experience enjoys putting people out of work with all the personal pain it causes. Clearly, the shareholders want the CEO to take whatever action is necessary to return the company to health, and often the market recognizes the value of their actions almost immediately. The individuals must be compensated for what they do. Otherwise, why would anyone be willing to make the hard decisions, to take the unpopular actions?

Naturally, the senior executives must take the public and employee relations impact of these actions into account. This may require that the plans be softened or handled somewhat differently to avoid the senior executives being perceived as greedy. Balancing all these issues is not trivial, but the stakes are high enough to make the effort.

VALUE AT THE TOP

Throughout the book I have been making two fundamental points:

First, despite its critics and its problems, there is an effectively operating labor market for key executives in the United States. CEOs lose their jobs, executives are promoted into top jobs, and they are recruited from other companies. Their annual incentives and cash compensation seem to move quite significantly with changes in their financial performance. Are there outlying companies, exceptions to this rule? Yes, and I urge the shareholders and boards of those companies to address the problem. There is some evidence that this pressure is working to rectify these exceptional companies. But as a general trend, there is broad-based pay for performance, especially in annual cash compensation for key executives.

Second, stock option plans—the primary type of long-term incentive among American corporations—motivate executives. However, given that the risk profile of a stock option holder is different from the risk profile of a real shareholder, a structural flaw, these plans do not motivate behaviors that are consistent with shareholder interests. Are there exceptions to this? Yes again, but as a general principal, as manifestations of the strategies chosen by executives who hold a lot of stock options, the executives choose strategies that are riskier than the shareholders apparently require.

Stock options have failed from two perspectives. They have not generated the significant stock ownership they were originally intended to produce. They have also failed in that, by holding on to the option itself, there is the break between executive and shareholder interests. Options motivate executives to undertake risky strategies, mainly acquisitions that are not in the shareholders' interests.

Corporations selected stock options in the past because they were the vehicle of choice. Board members probably had options at their own companies. It was the prudent thing to do for many companies—and it worked out for a number of companies whose risky strategies paid off. But it appears not to have paid off for an even larger number of companies.

The solution to this is to bypass the stock option as a vehicle to generate share ownership and to go directly to vehicles that require share ownership, such as purchased stock options, executive stock purchase, or some combination of these.

Requiring executives to have a more balanced profile of risk between themselves and shareholders is, I believe, in the long-term interests of all parties. The shareholders benefit. Employees benefit if the company becomes more stable and less likely to make bad acquisitions, to be taken over, and to require staff reductions and divestitures.

Finally, as I have argued throughout the book, I believe it is in the long-term interests of executives who are at all concerned with the long-term survival of their companies. Better long-term incentives will be to their advantage, in terms of job security and income maximization. They will benefit when their interests and the shareholder interests are joined through stock ownership.

APPENDIX

How to Evaluate Long-Term Incentive Values

THREE FACTORS influence the value of a long-term incentive award: (1) stock price performance; (2) market interest rates; and (3) executive behavior patterns. The Hay methodology of valuing the long-term incentive award addresses these factors through a two-step process.

First, we estimate the current dollar value of the gain that each grant will afford the executive as the grant vests. That is, we project the future value of the grant to the executive at time of payment, and then discount the payout back to the date of the grant to account for the time value of money and the risk that the plan will not pay out.

Second, we build in a discount based upon the probability of award forfeiture if the employee leaves the company. A 5 percent executive-level annual turnover rate assumption is applied over the average time for which the grant remains forfeitable, based on actual plan vesting provisions. For example, we will discount a performance unit plan that provides for full vesting after three years by 5 percent for three years, or 15 percent, while we will discount a similar plan vesting in three equal installments starting at the end of the first year by 5 percent for the average forfeiture period of two years $[(1+2+3)/3]$, or 10 percent.

For each executive, we apply the uniform two-step methodology to value long-term incentive grant data using the following assumptions:

Stock-based equity plans (restricted stock, performance shares, and phantom stock grants): We assume that common stock price represents the financial community's best estimate of the current value of an organization's securities, incorporating forecasts of both potential price growth and future dividend income. Therefore, we use fair market value at grant when estimating the current dollar value for equity plans that pay current or accrued dividend equivalents on underlying stock while the grant remains forfeitable.

For equity plans under which dividend equivalents are neither paid nor accrued, current value is assumed to be the fair market value at time of grant, less the projected present value of the dividend stream to which the executive is not entitled before the grant vests. This deduction for the present value of the unpaid dividend stream is calculated assuming that the most recent dividend paid will increase at an annual rate of 8 percent for the average period that the grant is forfeitable, and that the resulting future value should be discounted back to the time of grant based on the corporate annual prime rate of 10 percent.

Stock-based appreciation plans (stock options, stock appreciation rights, and phantom stock appreciation plans): To estimate these future gains, one must make assumptions about both future stock price performance and executive exercise behavior. To provide an unbiased projection of future gains, stock prices are assumed to grow at a uniform rate of 10 percent compounded annually, and stock options are assumed to be exercised at a uniform five years from the time of grant.

We can then discount projected gains back to the time of grant at the following annual discount rates that account for the time value of money, as well as the relative levels of risk associated with various plan types:

Incentive Stock Options (ISOs)	12%
Non-qualified Stock Options (NQSOs)	15%
Stock Appreciation Rights (SARs)	15%
Phantom Stock Appreciation Plans	15%

We further discount these current dollar values for the probability of award forfeiture as we described in the second step of our methodology.

Long-term incentive plans that do not use company stock (performance units, long-term cash): When we calculate current values, we assume that future payments will be made at 100 percent of target performance. We then discount the resulting gains by 10 percent annually, based on the corporate prime rate, to take into account the time value of money.

These current dollar values are further discounted for the probability of award forfeiture as described in step two.

Tandem plans: When we calculate totals across long-term incentive plan vehicles for grants issued in tandem (either/or basis), we assume the executive will exercise the grant with the highest present value.

The table below illustrates examples of the Hay Long-Term Incentive Valuation Methodology for some common vesting terms. For each example, the grant value is $100,000 and the annual dividend rate is 5 percent. Under the vesting provisions column, "3-year cliff" means that the stock, or whatever, vests 100 percent after three years. In other words, the executive falls off a cliff for the vesting. This is in contrast to "3-year installment," where the executive obtains one-third of the rights each year.

Cliff vesting has the advantage of greater retentive value than installment vesting. The executive who leaves two years and nine months into a cliff program gets nothing; under a three-year installment program, he'd have rights to two-thirds of the grant.

The figures indicate that, for example, under an incentive stock option (ISO) plan, the future value is $61,051, the current dollar value is $34,642, and the present value in 1991 is either $29,446 or $31,178, depending on the vesting provisions. Unpaid dividend equivalents are not applicable to ISO plans.

1991 Long-Term Incentive Valuation Methodology Examples

Plan Type	Vesting Provision	Future Value
ISO (Stock option)	3-Year Cliff	$61,051
	3-Year Installment	$61,051
NQSO (Stock option)	3-Year Cliff	$61,051
	3-Year Installment	$61,051
SAR	3-Year Cliff	$61,051
	3-Year Installment	$61,051
Restricted Stock	3-Year Cliff	N/A
With Dividend Equiva-lents	3-Year Installment	N/A
	3 Installments After 2 Years	N/A
Restricted Stock	3-Year Cliff	N/A
Without Dividend Equivalents	3-Year Installment	N/A
	3 Installments After 2 Years	N/A
Performance Share	3-Year Cliff	N/A
With Dividend Equiva-lents	3-Year Installment	N/A
	3 Installments After 2 Years	N/A
Performance Share	3-Year Cliff	N/A
Without Dividend Equivalents	3-Year Installment	N/A
	3 Installments After 2 Years	N/A
Performance Unit	3-Year Cliff	$100,000
	3-Year Installment	$100,000
Phantom Apprecia-tion	3-Year Cliff	$61,051
	3-Year Installment	$61,051
Phantom Grant Value + Appreciation	3-Year Cliff	N/A
	3-Year Installment	N/A

Grant Value = $100,000
Annual Dividend Rate = 0.05

SOURCE: The Hay Group.

Time Value Discount Factor	Current Dollar Value	Forfeiture Discount Factor	Unpaid Dividend Equivalents	1991 Present Value
0.567426	$34,642	.15	N/A	$29,446
0.567426	$34,642	.10	N/A	$31,178
0.497176	$30,353	.15	N/A	$25,800
0.497176	$30,353	.10	N/A	$27,318
0.497176	$30,353	.15	N/A	$25,800
0.497176	$30,353	.10	N/A	$27,318
N/A	$100,000	.15	N/A	$85,000
N/A	$100,000	.10	N/A	$90,000
N/A	$100,000	.15	N/A	$85,000
N/A	$100,000	.15	$14,145	$72,977
N/A	$100,000	.10	$ 9,616	$81,346
N/A	$100,000	.15	$14,145	$72,977
N/A	$100,000	.15	N/A	$85,000
N/A	$100,000	.10	N/A	$90,000
N/A	$100,000	.15	N/A	$85,000
N/A	$100,000	.15	$14,145	$72,977
N/A	$100,000	.10	$ 9,616	$81,346
N/A	$100,000	.15	$14,145	$72,977
0.751314	$75,131	.15	N/A	$63,862
0.826446	$82,645	.10	N/A	$67,616
0.497176	$30,353	.15	N/A	$25,800
0.497176	$30,353	.10	N/A	$27,318
N/A	$100,000	.15	N/A	$85,000
N/A	$100,000	.10	N/A	$90,000

BIBLIOGRAPHY

Bhagat, Sanjai et al. "Hostile Takeovers in the 1980s: The Return to Corporate Specialization." *Brookings Papers on Economic Activity* (1990): 1–84.

Bhide, Amar. "Reversing Corporate Diversification." *Journal of Applied Corporate Finance* (Summer 1990): 70–81.

Bremner, Brian. "Tough Times, Tough Bosses." *Business Week,* November 25, 1991, pp. 174–179.

Brickley, James A., Bhagat, Sanjai, and Lease, Ronald C. "The Impact of Long-Range Managerial Compensation Plans on Shareholder Wealth." *Journal of Accounting and Economics* 7 (1985): 115–130.

Byrne, John A. "The Flap over Executive Pay." *Business Week,* May 6, 1991, pp. 90–112.

Crystal, Graef S. "The Great CEO Sweepstakes." *Fortune,* June 18, 1990, pp. 94–102.

————. *In Search of Excess: The Over-Compensation of the American Executive.* W. W. Norton, 1991.

DeFusco, Richard A. et al. "The Association between Executive Stock Option Plan Changes and Managerial Decision Making." *Financial Management* (Spring 1991): 36–43.

Deutsch, Claudia H. "You Bet Your Check at Chrysler." *New York Times,* January 27, 1991.

Dunfee, Thomas W. *Business & Its Legal Environment.* Prentice Hall, 1987, p. 503.

Elliot, Margaret. "Redesigning Management Incentives." *Corporate Finance,* February 1990, pp. 32–37.

Fanning, Deirdre. "Bid-'em-up Bruce?" *Forbes,* August 7, 1989, p. 58.

Fuchsberg, Gilbert. "ITT Seeks to Tie Pay of Top Executives More Closely to Company's Performance." *Wall Street Journal,* September 13, 1991, p. B7.

"Gault on Fixing Goodyear's Flat." *Fortune,* July 15, 1991, pp. 104–105.

Goodman, Walter. "How 2 Parties Managed the S&L Bailout." *New York Times,* October 22, 1991, p. C18.

Henderson, Bruce D. *Henderson on Corporate Strategy.* New American Library, 1979.

Hofmann, Richard D. "The Restructuring of a Company on the Run." *Directors & Boards* (Winter 1989): 13–16.

Holderness, Clifford G., and Sheehan, Dennis P. "Raiders or Saviors? The Evidence on Six Controversial Investors." *Journal of Financial Economics,* April 1985, pp. 555–579.

Jensen, Michael. "CEO Roundtable on Corporate Stucture and Management Incentives." *Journal of Applied Corporate Finance* (Fall 1990): 6–35.

———. "Corporate Control and the Politics of Finance." *Journal of Applied Corporate Finance* (Summer 1991): 13–33.

———. "Eclipse of the Public Corporation." *Harvard Business Review,* September–October 1989, pp. 60–74.

———. "Takeovers: Their Causes and Consequences." *Journal of Economic Perspectives* (Winter 1988): 21–48.

Jensen, Michael, and Murphy, Kevin. "CEO Incentives—It's Not How Much You Pay But How." *Harvard Business Review,* May–June 1990, pp. 138–149.

Kaplan, Steven, "The Effects of Management Buyouts on Operating Performance and Value." University of Chicago Working Paper, August 1989.

Kay, Ira T. "Compensation Stategy: Matching Rewards to Risks." In *Handbook of Business Strategy,* edited by Harold Glass. Warren, Gorham & Lamont, 1991.

Kitching, John. "Early Returns on LBOs." *Harvard Business Review,* November–December 1989, pp. 74–81.

Klein, Michael R. "Skewered Shareholders: Roundtable on Time-Warner Deal." *Directors & Boards* (Winter 1990): 31.

Knowlton, Christopher. "11 Men's Million-Dollar Motivator." *Fortune,* April 9, 1990, pp. 65–67.

Kroll, Mark, Susan A. Simmons, and Peter Write. "Determinants of Chief Executive Office Compensation Following Major Acquisitions." *Journal of Business Research* 20 (1990): pp. 349–366.

Langbert, Mitchell. "In Search of Compensation: A Comparison of Executives in Peters and Waterman's Excellent and *Fortune*'s Least Admired Firms." *Benefits Quarterly* (Second Quarter 1990): 23–36.

Lewelleen, Wilber; Loderer, Kilido; and Rosenfeld, Ahron. "Merger Decisions and Executive Stock Ownership in Acquiring Firms." *Journal of Accounting and Economics* 7 (1985): 209–231.

Liebtag, W. "Compensating Executives." In *Executive Compensation,* edited by Fred K. Foulkes. Harvard Business School Press, 1991, pp. 27–42.

Macrae, Noman. "Wanted: Blue Bloods for American Boards." *Business Month,* April 1990, p. 16.

Mallory, Maria. "How Can We Be Laid off If We Own the Company?" *Business Week,* September 9, 1991, p. 64.

McConnel, John J., Purdue University, and Henri Servaes, University of Chicago. "Additional Evidence on Equity Ownership and Corporate Value," Working Papers, August 20, 1990.

Mitchell, Mark, and Lehn, Kenneth (Securities and Exchange Commission). "Do Bad Bidders Make Good Targets?" *Journal of Applied Corporate Finance* 3 (Summer 1990): 70–81.

Moore, Michael. "Compensation: The Million-Dollar-a-Year CEO Is Fast Becoming a Public Enemy." *Business Month,* October 1990, pp. 36–37.

Morck, Randall, Andrei Shleier, and Robert W. Vishny. "Characteristics of Targets of Hostile and Friendly Takeovers." In *Takeovers: Causes and Consequences,* edited by Alan J. Auerbach. University of Chicago Press, 1991.

Murphy, Kevin. "Top Executives Are Worth Every Nickle They Get." *Harvard Business Review,* March-April 1986, pp. 125–132.

Murray, Alan. "Bush's Rose Reflects Lack of Long View." *Wall Street Journal,* December 2, 1991, p. A-1.

Nelson-Horchler, Joani. "The Top Man Gets Richer." *Industry Week,* June 6, 1988, pp. 51–54.

Newman, George. "The Case for Obscene Salaries." *Across the Board,* September 1991, pp. 46–47.

Nye, Joseph S., Jr. *Bound to Lead: The Changing Nature of American Power.* Basic Books, 1990.

Rappaport, Alfred. "The Staying Power of the Public Corporation." *Harvard Business Review,* January-February 1990, pp. 96–104.

Roberts, Johnnie L. "Araskog, Confronted by ITT Holders, Defends $11.4 Million '90 Compensation." *Wall Street Journal,* May 8, 1991, p. A-3.

Rothchild, John. *Going for Broke.* Simon & Schuster, 1991.

Stewart, Bennett. *The Quest for Value,* HarperCollins, 1991, p. 76.

Stewart, Thomas A. "The Trouble with Stock Options." *Fortune,* January 1, 1990, pp. 93–95.

Tehranian, Hassan, and Waegelein, James F. "Market Reaction to Short-Term Executive Compensation Plan Adoption." *Journal of Accounting and Economics* 7 (1985): 131–144.

Working Group on Corporate Governance. "A New Compact for Owners and Directors." *Harvard Business Review,* July-August 1991.

Yago, Glen. *Junk Bonds.* Oxford University Press, 1991.

INDEX

Italics indicates tables or charts.

239